DON MATTINGLY'S

HITTING
IS SIMPLE

DON MATTINGLY'S

HITTING IS SIMPLE

The ABC's of Batting .300

DON MATTINGLY and JIM ROSENTHAL

With Photos by Tom DiPace

ST. MARTIN'S GRIFFIN
New York

www.stmartins.com

Photographs copyright © Tom DiPace

BOOK DESIGN BY AMANDA DEWEY

ISBN-10: 0-312-36620-5

ISBN-13: 978-0-312-36620-9

First Edition: March 2007

1 3 5 7 9 10 8 6 4 2

CONTENTS

ACKNOWLEDGMENTS

Special thanks to Ray Schulte and Kate Manchester at Ironclad Authentics—without their hard work and support this book could not have become a reality. Thanks to Tom DiPace, a great photographer and collaborator. Michael Homler and George Witte at St. Martin's always believed in this book, and for that the authors are much appreciative.

Rod Carew: When I was a kid I always wanted
to hit a baseball just like Rod Carew.
He was my baseball idol.

FOREWORD

I love to hit. I always have. Even now, more than twenty years after my 3,000th hit, I love to take a ball pitched to the outside part of the plate and lace it down the third baseline. And as easy as hitting sometimes appeared to be for me, I always get a laugh when people say I was a natural hitter. There is no such thing as a natural hitter. Sure, nature does play a part, but there is more nurture involved than there is nature.

No one understands this better than Don Mattingly. I was fortunate enough to meet Don when he was just coming up as a young player, and am happy to still consider him a friend. He has graciously credited me with being a positive influence on him, both as a hitter and as a model for how to comport yourself on and off the field. For that, I am honored.

Don and I have talked about hitting for hours. From those conversations I have come to know both the level and depth of Don's understanding of how to hit, and how to teach hitting. Don knows there is no magic bullet to being a good hitter. He knows that different situations in a game demand different approaches to hitting. For that very reason, you never saw Don Mattingly get himself out, or give away an at bat. Don understood that as personal as hitting is, sometimes it was more important to give yourself up to move a runner over than it was to selfishly try and be a hero. That's why he was a great hitter.

Don hated making an out, and he worked tirelessly to do everything possible to avoid making outs. Read his words carefully. Hear what he has to say. Practice what he preaches. He's accomplished everything in the batter's box that any player could ever hope to accomplish. Now it's your turn. Work hard and good luck.

—Rod Carew
 www.Rodcarew29.com

PREFACE

There is no better teacher of hitting than Don Mattingly. He has the information, intelligence, experience, and passion to give players—at all levels—what they need to be successful. When Don made the decision to coach at the major-league level for the New York Yankees I knew he'd be outstanding. He is very energetic. He has no problem handling an enormous workload. There's no limit on what he wants to learn and how he is able to communicate with the players. He would make a great major-league manager right now. He has no problem with the fear of failing—that's not even part of his vocabulary. Don has a fire burning inside of him to be the best, and to help others achieve their personal best. Don is always there for his players. And believe me, players in the big leagues right now demand so much more from their coaches because of the information that we get for them.

Don has at his fingertips all the information our players need: what a pitcher

Joe Torre: Character, class, and my baseball idol now that my playing days are over.

is likely to throw when he's ahead or behind in the count, his tendencies and patterns to try to get hitters out. But Don's value to the Yankees goes way beyond his teaching skills and value as a hitting coach. His personality is so good. It's almost like Donnie is still a player, to be honest, and that ability to banter with guys like Derek Jeter and Jorge Posada and Jason Giambi is an invaluable asset to me as a manager. Whatever your goals in baseball, Don Mattingly is the perfect source of information to get you headed in the right direction.

—Joe Torre
    Yankee Stadium
    August 2006

INTRODUCTION

My goal in writing this book is to help you to become a better hitter with simple, basic, and useful information. I'm not a hitting guru who claims to have all the answers. I'm just a hitting coach who has some good ideas and hands-on drills to help you to improve and to make steady progress. There are a lot of coaches with good information. But the learning process can get very complicated. I'm here to make life as simple as possible. The information in this book is a foundation to keep you focused on getting better through hard work and sound mechanics. Enjoy hitting and playing baseball to the best of your ability. Believe in yourself and be sure to have fun along the way.

The single most important part of becoming a good hitter—or even a great hitter—is saying to yourself before you step into the batter's box: "I'm going to get a hit against this pitcher. I'm not going to pull away from the ball. I will not be afraid. I will stay in there and put the bat on the ball. He is not getting me our or keeping me from hitting the ball hard somewhere."

All the mechanics and drills are secondary to you making this statement in your mind—"I can and I will get a hit against this pitcher!" If you want to take it to the next level, you must have this approach.

This is the one part of hitting that no coach can teach you. The best hitting coach in the world can't help you unless you have the mind-set that you will not give into that pitcher—you will not take no for an answer. And if you don't get it done, you must keep working and keep fighting until you do get it done the next time around.

As you keep reading this book we will always consider it a "win" when you get a good pitch to hit and you hit that pitch hard. If you can do that time in and time out you will be able to hit.

—Don Mattingly
Fall 2006

DON MATTINGLY'S

HITTING IS SIMPLE

THE FOUNDATION OF HITTING

Hitting .300 is as simple as learning the foundation of hitting. Coaches and instructors often make the mistake of complicating what is a very simple process. We tend to confuse kids by getting them to think about a bunch of technical jargon, when the basic foundation will do the job.

I'm going to give you a conventional and solid basis for everything you will do as a hitter, from day one. When you get to the higher levels—high school, college, and pro ball—and you are already pretty good, then it's okay to experiment with different stances if you think they will help you see the ball better.

To get started, here are all the basics of hitting that lay the groundwork for success:

BUILDING THE FOUNDATION

1. Start with the tool.

Swing a bat that feels comfortable to you. You don't want to grab a bat so heavy that it will force you to drag it through the strike zone, or one so light that it feels like a whiffle bat. Pick something that feels good. Get a bat in your hand that allows for a comfortable swing. We'll talk more about bats and batting gloves in chapter 2.

The bat must stay in your fingertips to get the hands moving free and easy.

Just before the pitch: The goal is to stay relaxed and ready to go.

2. The foundation is your stance.

When you stand in the batter's box, you want to be comfortable. I favor a shoulder-width stance for its simplicity and its ability to help me stay balanced. I always tell kids:

Make sure you are balanced on the balls of your feet, as this will allow you to swing the bat with consistency. The goal is to be able to take the bat from Point A to Point B. This movement starts with a simple stance.

3. The stride should also take you in a straight line.

If you were to draw a straight line from where your feet are aligned, the goal is to stride toward the pitcher. If I stride open—if I'm stepping back away from the pitcher—it will force my front-side shoulder to come out, and then I open my hips early. Next thing you know, I'm dropping my hands and I won't be able to take a straight path to the ball.

For me, the key to success is to take a straight path to the ball, to get back to basics. This first move causes a chain reaction. If you follow that straight path, your hips stay square and at that point you can take the bat directly to the ball.

Remember that the shortest distance between two points (from the bat to

(From left to right): Once again, I'm staying relaxed until the pitcher is ready. As the pitcher is getting started I pick my hands up and get ready to start my swing. The swing gets started with a slight shift of weight to the backside.

the ball) is a straight line. Any deviation from the straight line will make your swing longer. That's when you hear comments like "He is dragging his bat through the strike zone."

You do see guys with long swings make it to the big leagues, and they tend to be power hitters who strike out a lot. Their swing is not as consistent; they are more hot and cold–type hitters.

Ideally, you want a shorter swing that goes directly from Point A to Point B because shorter is quicker. If pitchers throw harder, a longer swing will give you less time to make a decision. We're talking about time and distance: A swing on a straight line puts your hands straight to the path of the pitch. If you have a longer swing, though, your path is not quite as direct and that little movement will end up causing you trouble.

4. Put the bat on your shoulders to start the hands.

Now that we've talked about the feet being fairly straight in the stance and the stride moving in a straight line, the next element is proper hand position. My advice is to lay the bat on your shoulders; as you pick the bat up, your hands are in a solid position to hit the baseball. The goal is to get your hands in a nice, relaxed position to start the swing.

Summary

You want to have a shoulder-width stance; a good, balanced position, aligned with the release point—the zone around which a pitcher will release the baseball; and your hands in a nice, relaxed position on the bat.

5. You have to go back to go forward.

This rule applies to almost any athletic activity. The objective is to create some type of momentum. A cat that's on the prowl is in a coiled position before it strikes—same thing with a snake that's coiled. They are essentially moving in reverse—before striking at their prey.

For hitting, there needs to be a little bit of lean back to initiate the swing before you stride forward. You'll see some hitters do a little step back, which is often called the "toe-tap." Chipper Jones of the Atlanta Braves does this, and it works well for him: He steps back and then goes forward. I don't teach the toe-tap, but you have to do something in your swing to get your weight to go back before you move forward—and obviously it works for Chipper.

Think of this triggering mechanism as a bow and arrow: You have to draw back the bow slowly and then let it go so that the arrow can hit its target. Same thing with hitting: It's a slow start to your swing, with a lean to trigger the movement—the coiling of the snake—and then a smooth move forward. As you pick up your front foot, you should be able to stand on one leg or move forward or glide toward the ball under control. If I pick up my front foot and fall forward, it's a sure bet that my balance is off.

(From left to right): A side view of the swing: Take a slight movement back to initiate the swing. You should now be able to stay balanced on the back leg, so as you move back and your front foot comes off the ground you will be able to stand in at the plate in a comfortable, ready position.

Here's how it all works together in sequence: I'm relaxed and ready as I step into the batter's box with a shoulder-width stance. I've got the bat in the position where I picked it up off my shoulders, the pitch is coming, I pick up my foot, and I have to go back before going forward or I'll be unbalanced at the outset of the swing.

6. Weight transfer=keep your head down on the ball.

Shift, carry, and glide your weight from back to middle to the point of contact as you keep your head and eyes down on the ball. Swing down on the ball as if you're chopping down a tree with an ax—taking the knob to the ball, keeping the barrel of the bat above the hands.

7. Finish your swing.

I prefer "finish your swing" to the concept of the "follow-through" on the swing. You always hear about "staying through the ball," and that simply means to leave your head down and finish your swing. Don't look up to find out where the ball went. It feels natural, but it cuts your swing off. The goal is to hit *through* the ball and then look for it after making contact.

When you hear baseball coaches talk about "to it and through it" all they really mean is to finish the swing. *Swing to the ball and swing through the ball.* If you are trying to chop down a tree with an ax, you never stop short at the point of contact. You want to chop as if you are cutting all the way through that tree.

It's the same deal with swinging a baseball bat. If you stop the swing and

As you start the swing (four photos above) the goal is to work down on the ball, which leaves the bat flat in the strike zone. Again, we want to finish the swing before we look up for the baseball to assure that we swing all the way through the ball.

look up as soon as you hit the ball, you end up falling backward. Now, if you swing through the ball, your transfer of weight keeps you going. You'll rotate through the ball and finish your swing.

8. How deep in the batter's box to stand.

This is a personal deal. I liked being in the very back of the box. My feeling was that the back of the box gave me more time to see the ball and make adjustments.

Tony Gwynn would always stand in the middle of the box, with his front foot in front of the plate and his back foot in back of the plate. Other players like being even with the plate.

Some hitters will move up in the box to hit the breaking ball. But Tony Gwynn will tell you that moving up or back in the box is the biggest mistake you can make—he was a creature of habit, and preached staying in a comfort zone that's predictable every time you hit, so you know what to expect.

Like I said, I would always stay on the back *line* of the box, but I would move closer to or farther away from the plate depending on who was pitching. I would move closer to the plate against a pitcher like Jamie Moyer, who throws a good change-up and specializes in off-speed pitches. That kind of pitcher likes a lot of room, and that's why I would stand as close to the plate as possible and force everything to be right in my hitting zone. I do not want off-speed pitchers to have any space to throw the ball from inside to outside; if he wants to come inside, a guy like Moyer would almost have to hit me with the pitch.

If, however, I was facing a power pitcher like Randy Johnson, I would move farther away from the plate to give him more room—not because he's going to hit me, but because I want to cover only one half of the plate or the other. I'm not going to try to cover the entire plate against a power pitcher. I'm only going to hit those pitches that are going to end up being strikes on the inner half of the plate. If Randy can throw two strikes on the outside corner, he'll have me in a 0–2 hole, and now I'm going to have to fight to get a hit. But up until I'm in that 0–2 hole, I'm still going to try to cover half the plate.

As I reach for the outside part of the plate, the goal is to be able to touch the outside corner; if you bend your knees, you should always have proper plate coverage. A solid swing that is fundamentally sound will enable you to adjust to a wide variety of pitches and locations.

9. Plate coverage

If you don't stride straight and stay balanced, you're going to have a lot of trouble making contact against a lot of different pitches. You may still be able to hit a pitch that's on the inside corner because that's in a zone you can still reach, but most of the time you will hit that pitch foul. Now you know why I favor solid, straight-line mechanics, as they allow you to hit more pitches in more zones of the plate.

Your mission is to learn how to hit in a way that allows you to handle more pitches from a variety of styles of pitchers. A solid swing that is fundamentally sound will enable you to adjust to a wide variety of pitches and locations. Pulling off the pitch or having a long swing will make it very tough for you to hit pitches in certain areas of the plate. The mechanics of your swing will often dictate what pitches you can and cannot hit. Many hitters never figure out how to hit pitches in all locations, but they're smart enough to lay off the pitches they can't handle and instead focus on the pitches they can hit. You either learn to hit a certain pitch or you quit swinging at it—that's the mark of a smart hitter.

Remember that very few pitchers have pinpoint control. If a pitcher can throw the ball where he wants to all the time, he's going to win almost every battle—assuming, of course, his stuff matches up with his precision. Every hitter has holes in his swing; it comes down to whether the pitcher has the control needed to locate his pitches with consistency.

10. Avoid overstriding or lunging at the pitch.

If you stride too far, your head starts to move and you won't get a good look at the pitch.

11. The inside-out swing—your hands lead the bat head.

An inside-out hitter keeps his hands inside the baseball. It's a great way to look at what Tony Gwynn talks about, when he says to "Take the knob of the bat to the ball." You can still pull the pitch but you have to keep your hands inside the ball, so your swing must be short and compact.

I like the concept of the inside-out swing, or hands inside the ball, because it keeps a player focused on the straight-line mechanics that are the foundation of hitting. Let's say you get a pitch to hit in the middle part of the plate. If you have a good swing—and you are making sure your hands are inside of the ball, you can hit the ball in any of three or four different places and it will look as if you hit the ball on the nose. You can hit a bullet to left-center, a bullet to dead center, a bullet to right-center, and probably hard down either line. In each case, it would look like you hit the ball right on the nose.

12. Sound mechanics will allow you to hit the ball to all fields.

Remember that you have to hit the ball where it's pitched; that's basic. So the one solid swing we've been working on will allow you to hit the ball to left field, center field, or right field.

The hands go back slowly; you go directly to the ball; and you hit it in different spots, depending on the location of the pitch, to spray the ball to all fields.

The pitch that nips the outside corner has to come farther to you, and so you'll have to hit it back farther, or deeper, toward you at the plate. A left-handed batter will shoot that pitch toward the left; a right-handed hitter will shoot that pitch toward the right. The ball you hit up the middle is a ball you hit a little farther out in front of you, and it's located toward the middle part of the plate.

Pulling the ball is the last thing you'll learn, and it is the toughest thing to do properly because you have to hit the ball so far out in front. You'll still be able to keep your hands inside the ball that's on the inside part of the plate, but you've got to hit it farther out—you have to stay closed longer, to get to that pitch and pull it to the left or right.

2

BATS AND GRIPS AND GLOVES

Don Mattingly always understood the right way to swing the bat. He knew how to use the tools of the trade to his advantage. And he never wasted an at bat—he made every pitch count.

—CAL RIPKEN, JR.

Bobby Abreu: As he finishes his swing, he's looking up for the ball in perfect balance.

The only way to apply the solid foundation of hitting is with a fluid, controlled, and relaxed swing. That's a given, and yet one of the biggest problems facing young and old hitters is that they grip the bat way too tight.

All this talk about proper mechanics and the foundation of hitting goes out the window if you are squeezing the bat instead of applying a relaxed grip. Let the bat feel loose in your hands so that the wrist action is like casting a fishing line or popping a whip. Casting a fishing line calls for a flick of the wrist. The same flick-of-the-wrist technique applies to swinging a baseball bat.

Study and analyze the hitting style of Bobby Abreu of the Yankees, to appreciate a relaxed approach. Bobby has no unnecessary movement in his swing to take away from that straight-line and bottom-hand-to-the-ball swing. And he is consistent with that flick-of-the-wrist motion to produce bat speed and fluidity.

Remember that the goal is to find a bat that's not too heavy or too light. We want a bat that feels comfortable in our hands.

SELECTING THE RIGHT BAT

The length and weight of the bat are two important variables that allow a hitter to develop a relaxed, smooth, quiet swing.

1. Judging bat weight:

This is comparable to testing the weight of a suitcase. You know how, when you pick up a bag that has too much stuff crammed into it, it feels too heavy when you lift it off the floor? The goal is to pack a bag that you can carry comfortably when running to catch a flight. Same thing with a wet, soggy baseball—you try to throw it and somehow it just doesn't feel right in your hand because it's too heavy for proper mechanics. Pick a bat that's comfortable for both its weight and length. You don't want a bat that's so heavy it will drag through the zone.

The right weight will enable you to extend the barrel of the bat out over the plate to hit bullets to all fields. Many players favor light bats to get a sense of control and to improve contact.

Another line drive from Tony Gwynn. Notice the head position—head and eyes down on the ball.

TONY GWYNN: *I discovered the light bat when I was playing at San Diego State University, and where I now coach the baseball team. Before going to college I used any bat that was available—I wasn't too picky.*

I hit .301 my sophomore year at SDSU—not bad, but nothing special if the goal is to get drafted and play pro ball. I just kind of viewed it as a shaking off the rust from skipping baseball during my freshman year.

Coming back the next season, I immediately got thrown into the batting cage to work on my stroke. My old aluminum model from sophomore year (34 inches, 32 ounces) had a big dent in it, so I had to find a new bat.

I went into the cupboard at the San Diego State University locker room. I was looking around, and found this little 32-inch, 31-ounce bat. I pulled it off the rack and just fiddled with it in my hands and thought, "This bat feels so good; I wonder if I can hit with this thing?"

So I brought it into the batting cage, and right away I'm stinging the ball. I'm hitting line drives all over the place. From that point on, I was more conscious of the weight and length of the bat. I suddenly began to notice the bat size used by the other guys on the team. A typical light aluminum model was 34 inches and 29 ounces—that's a big difference

The plan is to head to the plate with a bat that builds confidence. Consistency is the key to success. It doesn't matter if the pitcher is right-handed or left-handed, a flame-thrower or a soft-tosser; either way, you want the same swing and the same solid approach every time.

between weight and length—while my bat, at 32 inches and 31 ounces, had a much closer ratio of inches to ounces.

The other players were getting "whip action" with the longer bat, but there wasn't enough weight in it to have a positive impact on their swing.

The moral of that story is that you want to find a bat that feels right to you the first time you pick it up and test it out. A bat that's too light can do more harm than good. You want to swing a bat that has enough weight to drive the ball and to make consistent contact.

2. Changing bats to break out of slumps:

I would do this only by chance, not by design. There's nothing wrong with trying new bats if they feel right to you. I'd pick up a bat from Willie Randolph by mistake and think, "This thing feels good." And so I'd use it in games for a couple of days with varying degrees of success. A different bat gives you a different feel. But it's funny how, a day or two later, you want to go back to your own bat—the one that worked for you over time.

Don't make a conscious decision to swing a new bat when you're in a slump. You might be messing around with another bat and give it a try, but that's not the plan typically to break out of a slump.

The plan is to head to the plate with a bat that builds confidence. Consistency is the key to success. It doesn't matter if the pitcher is right-handed or left-handed, a flamethrower or a soft-tosser; either way, you want to use the same swing and the same solid approach every time. And that means using the same bat, whose weight gives you a sense of control.

For an ideal grip, you want the bat in your fingertips to allow for proper use of your hands. The V-grip bat is the perfect way to allow kids to understand and apply the concept of putting the bat in the fingertips and lining up the knuckles.

GRIPPING THE BAT—THE CREATION OF THE V-GRIP DESIGN

Grip is the key to success or failure with any bat. When I was coaching my kids back in Evansville, Indiana, I noticed that they would always squeeze the bat too hard rather than apply a relaxed grip. What's more, kids can't understand the concept of putting the bat in the fingertips and lining up the knuckles. For proper knuckle alignment, you want to line up the middle knuckles of your fingers on both hands.

I started wondering about the possibility of a bat design that would automatically set the right knuckle alignment and fingertip grip.

The Evolution of the V-Grip Bat

It all started when a company came to spring training one year and they had made a bat with an ax-handle grip. I loved the way it felt in my hands. It put the bat right in my fingers, and I was a guy who had a tendency to press the bat back against my thumb; I wore a thumb guard to actually push the bat into my fingers. All hitting instructors talk about the need to get the bat into your fingers. It's an essential element of a proper grip to swing a bat with that relaxed swing we strive for.

Unfortunately, the bat this company produced with the ax-handle grip was like hitting with a two-by-four. The back part of the bat had that grip so it was almost square—it just buried my thumb, so it was impossible to use in game situations.

I filed this bat idea away for many years without giving up on the goal to produce a bat that would line up the knuckles and protect the thumbs from punishment.

I had retired from baseball and was living in Evansville, raising horses and enjoying spending time with my family, when one day a friend of mine—Jerry "Peanut" Gaines, a sheriff from Bowling Green, Kentucky—stopped by to tell me he knew a carpenter who wanted to show me a special bat. I wasn't interested in his bat but he clearly knew how to work with wood, so I had a good idea: I asked him to make a bat that would automatically put the knuckles and fingertips in the right place. He came back two weeks later with a prototype; we tweaked the design, and it was pretty nice. I started hitting with it a little bit, just to try it out, to see if I was going to hurt my thumb and figure out if it fit right in the fingertips. I liked it! I asked him to make me a few of these bats for the kids, so they could give it a try, and I also had him make some shorter bats (30 inch) for short-bat drills.

That's how Mattingly Baseball got started. Once we had the prototypes figured out, we got a patent and decided to move forward with the idea of making bats to get more kids to try this new design. It's funny because I started this company out of a simple idea to help my kids use their hands better on the bat, to make hitting easier and more comfortable. But you put the bat in your hand and the first thought that pops in your head is, "This is perfect. It fits right in the fingertips. You don't have to think about what you're doing; the bat does everything for you."

COMFORT, GRIP, AND BATTING GLOVES

The V-bat is a useful tool to improve your grip on the bat in much the same way that batting gloves protect your hands from injury and slipping off of the bat. I didn't start wearing batting gloves until I was drafted by the New York Yankees and shipped out to Oneonta in the New York–Penn League. Part of my reason for going with batting gloves was the switch from aluminum bats in high school to wooden bats in pro baseball.

With aluminum bats, you don't have as much of a need to wear batting gloves.

If your hands get all sweaty in the hot, humid summer weather, then batting gloves would make sense to give you a firm grip. If you don't feel comfortable with the batting gloves, though, you should not force yourself to wear them just because you think it's the right thing to do. It all comes down to comfort and grip.

Keep in mind that, whichever bat you use, batting gloves will protect your hands from blisters, injury, and discomfort over a long season of games, practice, and drills.

All players have their own likes and dislikes in glove design. I prefer gloves that fit tight, with no loose fabric hanging off the end of the fingers. Look for gloves that are perfectly aligned to the contours of your hands; excess fabric will move around on your hand while you swing the bat.

ALUMINUM BATS VS. WOODEN BATS

There's no question that you have to make an adjustment when going from aluminum to wood. I believe that you are better off learning to hit with a wooden bat; you can *feel* it when you hit the ball dead on the nose. With aluminum, you can hit the ball a long way even if you hit the ball on the label or all the way down on the handle. In other words, with aluminum, you can make mistakes and still hit the ball hard.

But the popularity of aluminum bats has more to with economics than performance. With aluminum, you can be sure that you'll use only one bat the entire baseball season. But I favor practicing with wood, in the hitting drills that we'll discuss in chapter 5.

A college player at U. Miami using an aluminum bat; even if you play with aluminum at your school, you would benefit by practicing with wood bats.

Advantages of Aluminum

An aluminum bat virtually takes away the ability for a pitcher to bust you inside. He can jam you with that inside pitch and, thanks to your aluminum bat, you'll still be able to do something good and make contact.

Aluminum bats have created a generation of hitters who dive out over the plate and a generation of sinkerball specialists who try to induce batters to swing at pitches in the dirt.

In college baseball, you see a lot of hitters who dive out over the outside pitch; they can go the other way with authority and hit with power to the opposite field, but they can't handle the inside pitch. And by the time they make it to pro ball, it's an adjustment to face a pitcher who knows how to pitch inside. The truth is, you have to go back to basics when you switch from aluminum to wood, as the days of getting by on those aluminum-bat fluke hits are long gone.

CARING FOR YOUR BAT

Rod Carew, my role model and my baseball hero while I was growing up in Indiana, always talked about the importance of taking care of your bats. Experiment with pine tar, tape, or stickum on the handle. Try different combinations to figure out what will work best for a firm grip.

I preferred a first baseman's glove that was just a little bit longer than average—a long-and-narrow scoop-style glove.

FIELDING GLOVES AND PERSONAL PREFERENCE

Selecting the right bat or the perfect glove all comes down to what works best for your game. Keith Hernandez, the top fielding first baseman in the National League while I was playing in the American League in the eighties, used a different model than I did. The decision boils down to what works best for your style of play, but the key is to take care of your glove so it will last a long time.

My model was even bigger than Keith's "Big Dipper," as I preferred a long-and-narrow scoop-style first baseman's glove. It's a personal deal.

Notice Keith Hernandez' balance: He has already hit the ball, and yet he is still in balance as he's taking off to run to first base.

BALANCE IS EVERYTHING IN BASEBALL

Keith was a great clutch hitter for the St. Louis Cardinals and the New York Mets. His greatness as a fielder was based on balance, quickness, reflex response and intelligence. He was able to field bunts on the third-base side of the diamond and throw runners out at third. That was more of a National League–type of play back in the eighties. He was able to cheat over to third and make those incredible plays on guys who had a rep as good bunters (there were fewer good bunters in the American League in the eighies).

Keith and I used to put one leg in foul territory while holding a runner on at first. As a left-handed-throwing first baseman, I squared up to take a throw over from the pitcher. This "squaring up" is very much the same as the correct approach to hitting—if you are trying to hold a runner on and you have both feet in fair territory and you are also trying to tag the runner, well, on a bad throw you can't maneuver. So to be square, I wanted one foot outside of the line in foul territory while I could look directly at the pitcher.

The whole game of baseball is based on being in balance—fielding, running, and hitting all depend on balance, and that's what will determine your progress and success in everything you do on the baseball field.

3

HARD WORK BREEDS SUCCESS

Donnie is a great coach because he's willing to put the time and effort into helping his players. I don't know where I'd be without him at my side.

—JASON GIAMBI

Before you learn how to become a .300 hitter, you must make a commitment to two things: working hard and having fun. If you enjoy playing the game, it's no big deal to spend an hour hitting off the batting tee, taking soft toss or batting practice, or fielding ground ball after ground ball to get better.

In all the years I played professional baseball, I never met a player who didn't have to work hard to be successful. But what's the point of learning a skill if you don't get enjoy what you're doing? It has to be something that you love, that you have a passion for—and forget the shortcuts.

You have to put the time, effort, and concentration into getting better at any skill. That's basic. But you must have a passion for that skill, sport, or activity. Without passion, you will never have the competitive fire that allows you to get better and better.

I like this photo because you can tell that I hit the ball the opposite way—my balance is solid.

MAKING THE COMMITMENT TO BASEBALL

I was a three-sport athlete in high school and loved to compete to win. Besides being on the baseball team, I excelled at basketball and football, while I also played tennis and racquetball. I enjoyed all of these sports and had no plan to pursue a career in baseball until the summer of my freshman year in high school.

I was fifteen years old and damn lucky to be on an excellent American Legion baseball team in Evansville, Indiana, that even included some college players. Back in the seventies each American Legion post had the pick of the best players from the top four or five high school programs in the area, and the competition was intense. There was a kid by the name of Mark King who was pitching against us for Kentucky—we had a pretty good rivalry going in American Legion ball between teams in Kentucky and Indiana.

The Kentucky–Indiana game was the night before King signed his deal with the Cincinnati Reds, and a huge crowd from two states watched Indiana win 2–1. I went 2-3 with a couple of doubles against King. And that one ball game was the beginning of my commitment to baseball.

All of a sudden I was receiving letters from big-league scouts, on official letterhead. I can tell you that it's pretty exciting to open your mail as a teenager and see the logo of the Cincinnati Reds or New York Yankees.

As each baseball season would roll around, I'd work on building hand strength with wrist exercises, and hit in the cage and in the practice and in games. I loved every minute of high school baseball. I had a coach in Quentin Merkel who was a work-oriented guy.

And the hard work paid off with winning a state championship when I was a junior (the team went 30–0). We lost in the state championship game the following season, with a 29–1 record—we had won fifty-nine games in a row before that loss in the title game. After the 30–0 season, a lot of coaches would have been smug and satisfied, but he challenged each player to get better and work harder:

"If you feel like you're the best player in town, strive to become the best player in your region. If you feel like you're the best player in your region, strive to become the best player in Indiana. If you feel like you're the best player in Indiana, strive to become the best player in the nation."

On June 5, 1979, the New York Yankees selected me in the nineteenth round of the amateur draft. I signed right out of high school. When I look back on it and reflect on my skills, here is what the scouts were looking at when they dropped me down to the nineteenth round:

- My arm strength was below average for an outfielder.
- My power was well below average for a top prospect.
- I was a singles hitter who hit mostly to the opposite field.

It would have taken a skilled scout to have been able to project that all of those tools would improve over time, with hard work and dedication.

The hidden x-factor in drafting a prospect is: How motivated is this player to be his best? Most teams could not have guessed how hard I was willing to work to make it to the big leagues. Major-league organizations spend more time researching this type of intangible element now than they did when I was drafted. They ask questions like: What kind of kid is this? Does he work hard? Is he able to make adjustments? Would he be willing to learn a new position and work hard at being good?

It is a fine line between success and failure. The talent pool is so close that a lot of guys have the capability and talent to make it to the top. The thing that sets these prospects apart is the commitment to working hard physically and mentally, and to understand the nuances of the game.

THE TRANSITION TO PRO BASEBALL

I had an easy transition, going from high school to pro ball. I got to play baseball every night and hang around during the day. I thought it was the best thing to do in the whole world. And I was even getting paid to play a game that I loved.

There were several roving hitting instructors in the Yankee organization when I first arrived, but the person who made the biggest impression on me was Mickey Vernon, a former first baseman with the Philadelphia Phillies.

Mickey was great for me because he wasn't the kind of batting coach who tried to make major changes in my swing. He would simply watch what I was doing in the cage, and it was often unclear what he was thinking. But I remember something he said at the time that made a big impression: "Donnie, don't let

I prefer batting gloves that fit tight, with no loose fabric hanging off the end of the fingers. Look for gloves that are perfectly aligned to the contours of your hands.

anyone tell you that you can't play in the major leagues just the way you are as a hitter right now." He gave me confidence that I could make it to the big leagues, even if I didn't have much power for a first baseman–outfielder. He wasn't telling me I had it made right then and there, without putting in even more hard work. All he was saying was that I shouldn't let anyone take away my God-given gift that I had developed to put the barrel of the bat on the ball.

MICKEY VERNON: *I met Donnie for the first time in 1979. He was playing for Oneonta in short-season Class A, the first rung of the ladder in the New York Yankees farm system. Donnie impressed me right away with his bat control. He made good contact and was spraying the ball all over the field.*

The following season, the Yankees sent him to Greensboro, North Carolina, to work on playing left field. I can tell you that his hitting was already very good.

My theory on hitting instruction is that you should watch a young hitter to figure out what the scouts saw in him in the first place. After you evaluate a player, then—and only then—would you consider making a change in his swing or his batting stance. My rule is to adjust and fine-tune rather than change what made the kid a good hitter from the get-go. Donnie didn't need to be told too much because he had the natural ability to put the bat on the ball.

Then I went to Columbus [AAA] to help Donnie with his fielding at first base and with his hitting, which was pretty darn good. I remember sending a report on him to the Yankees that year [1982], in which I described him as a future All-Star who would lead the league in batting one year [Mattingly won the AL batting title in 1984 with a .343 mark]. I also said he was capable of hitting fifteen to twenty home runs, once he

*Signing autographs is a great way to get close to the kids.
It's a part of the game!*

learned how to pull the ball [Mattingly hit more than twenty home runs five times during his thirteen-year major-league career].

Look at the numbers! He had a tremendous swing and a great career because of how hard he worked to improve, evolve, and adjust.

I remember working with him on his fielding at first base: I'd organize infield drills, where I'd hit the ball to certain spots and he'd have to run over to the first-base bag, turn, and make an accurate, strong throw to second base. He would work for hours to improve his fielding, and ultimately he became the best first baseman in the American League for the better part of a decade.

Donnie is a great role model for kids. His experience and intelligence makes him a great teacher of hitting, and he's a terrific person and a hard worker to go along with his skill and talent. You do have to work hard to get to the major leagues—trust me—and Donnie worked for all the success he enjoyed in his career.

I remember also working with Rex Hudler, a teammate of Donnie's in Greensboro, and "Hud" and all of the other young players knew that Donnie was a very special player.

REX HUDLER: *Donnie and I played together in the New York Yankees farm system. He was a nineteenth-round pick, and I was a first-round pick a year later [1980], and yet Donnie made it to New York before I did. By the time I got to the Yankees in 1984, Donnie had a rock concert going on—he was the best hitter in baseball from 1984 to '89.*

But in those early days in the low minors, the thing that set Donnie apart was the kind of person that he was. He would look at me, shake his head, and tell me: "Hud—you are going to be a big leaguer." His wife, Kim, was very nice, too, and I was so happy for both of them when Don was called up at the end of the 1982 season.

The thing you can learn from Donnie is that he had to work hard to learn how to pull the ball and hit to all fields with power. When he signed, he was figured on as an outfielder. But with hard work he turned himself into a Gold Glove first baseman. He had soft hands, a big first baseman's glove, and an intense competitive desire to be the best

It looks like another good swing from Rex "The Hud Dog" Hudler. It looks like he's hit the ball well, his head is down, and he's in balance.

4

GETTING BETTER WITH EXPERIENCE

Don Mattingly was a great hitter because he learned something new from every game he played.

—WILLIE RANDOLPH

I learned more about the mechanics of the swing
from Lou Piniella than anyone else I ever worked
with—he taught me how the swing works
and how to make adjustments.

After spending time with Mickey Vernon, I began to gain a lot of confidence in my swing. Lou Piniella, a legendary figure with the New York Yankees teams under manager Billy Martin, was the next guy to have a big impact on my success. Lou was hanging around the batting cage during my first spring training with the Yankees, watching me swing the bat, and told me to use my bottom hand to generate power and to pull the ball more.

Lou was still playing at this point, and he later became a successful hitting coach and manager for several teams. He took the time to show me how to use the bottom hand in my swing; this shred of instructional advice was the last piece of the puzzle for me in my learning curve from a good prospect to a major-league hitter.

HOW TO USE THE BOTTOM HAND—THE KEY IS TO GET ON TOP OF THE BALL

As a left-handed hitter, my stronger hand was my top hand. I had always heard about "getting on top of the ball," and I looked at the statement to mean quite literally to "hit the top of the baseball." Now, that would mean to keep the barrel above the ball and above your hands. So if you swing down into the ball, it is like swinging an ax down into a tree.

For the most part, you want the swing to begin in a downward path; your hands are around your ears or shoulders, and let's say the upper part of the strike zone is a little bit higher than your belt. And so the bat is coming down on the ball, and you are swinging through the ball to finish the swing.

If the pitch is inside or sinking, you still want to use the bottom hand to get down on the ball. This bottom-hand work creates backspin, and that's how my power jumped to the point where I could hit more than thirty home runs for the Yankees.

Lou Piniella's message was simple: I should use my bottom hand to try to hit down on the top half of the ball, to hit line drives and grounders, but the net effect was to increase my power by using my bottom hand more to correct and improve the swing, grounded in the simple foundation we built in chapter 1.

TROUBLESHOOTING TIPS

1. Avoid Strikeouts.

I was always taught that with two strikes in the count, I should cut my swing back a little bit or even choke up on the bat to shorten my swing.

If you put the ball in play, you can make something good happen: You might hit a roller through the hole or hit a flare over the infield. The shortstop might bobble a hard grounder. If you don't hit the ball, you have absolutely no chance of helping your team.

The game has changed a lot since I was playing in the eighties and nineties. My generation of players, guys like Willie Randolph, were embarrassed to strike out as much as the hitters do today.

I believe there's validity to the value of any hitter cutting down his swing to make contact with two strikes. If you put the ball in play, you've got a better chance to help your team.

Fall back on the foundation we built in chapter 1: A square (square = straight line to the ball) stance; a square stride, with the bottom hand going to the ball; movement from Point A to Point B. This is the foundation for a shorter swing that will cut down on your strikeouts and improve your ability to make contact with consistency.

It looks like a need a shave and an attitude adjustment in this photo.

2. Focus on the Pitcher.

The best way for a young hitter to prepare is to watch the pitcher. Pay attention when he's warming up before the game. Check out his delivery and stuff while you're standing in the on-deck circle or sitting in the dugout. Get an idea about what kind of stuff he has and whether he's throwing strikes.

Pay attention and watch!

That's true of so many things in this game. Pay attention to what's going on right in front of you. Don't let your mind wander and start thinking about where you're going to eat after the game. Try to use the time in the on-deck circle to your advantage. Consider all the things the pitcher may try to do to get the better of you.

3. Coordinate the Release Points with Your Hitting.

Nothing ever happens without the baseball! If you always know where the ball is, you will never get in any trouble. This is true whether you're running the bases, playing defense, or trying to find the release point (the point at which the pitcher is releasing the baseball from his hand).

It's that simple, really. Coaches get so complicated, trying to force kids to think about where their hands and feet are going on the swing. Once you are playing a game, the focus must be on seeing the ball. Keep your head as still as possible. You don't want a lot of movement when the pitcher delivers the baseball, or it will make it harder to read the ball coming out of his hand.

Your eyes need to be able to give you useful information. Once the pitch comes out of his hand, I want you to focus on the ball. Some pitchers will tip their pitches by throwing fastballs straight over the top or breaking balls with a three-quarter delivery. The change in delivery may tell you what pitch he's throwing.

But you can't achieve anything as a hitter unless you can see the baseball. Always study a pitcher as he is getting ready to start his windup. Follow him with your eyes as he goes into his stretch.

The goal as a hitter is to try to find the spot where a pitcher is releasing the baseball (middle photo). Once the pitch comes out of his hand, I want you to focus on the ball. Always study a pitcher as he is getting ready to start his windup. Follow him with your eyes as he goes into his stretch.

Don't let all sorts of extra motion in his delivery throw you off track in analyzing what pitch he's throwing. Stay in the box, don't abandon your solid foundation, and by studying the pitcher you will be able to find his release point and hit the ball.

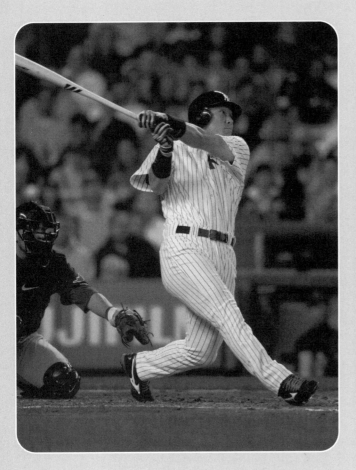 

4. Hit the Breaking Ball.

Making adjustments at the plate fits in with the whole idea of keeping hitting as simple as possible. The foundation we've been talking about creates a straight and smooth stride—without unnecessary head movements; a direct path to the pitch; and perfect balance. That means you are never moving forward until you move back. Your eyes will focus on the baseball coming from the release point. And you will be able to see the breaking ball and the fastball and the change-up.

Early on in my career, I struggled against soft-tossing pitchers, the guys who changed speeds effectively. I had to learn how to adjust my thinking dur-

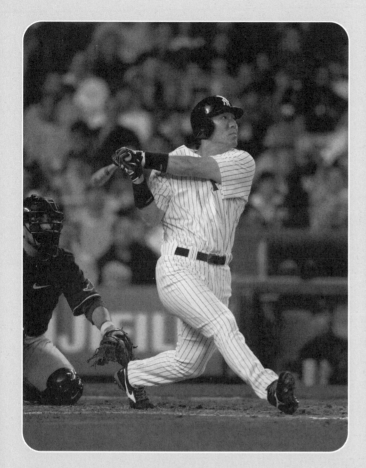

(Left to right): Hideki Matsui is a great breaking-ball hitter; notice how his head stays still during the swing. Remember to be true to the foundation of the swing when hitting a breaking ball—no unnecessary head movement, a direct path to the pitch, and perfect balance.

ing the at bat. This ability to make adjustments is a skill that only comes with experience. After facing guys who change speeds, you will formulate a plan to sit back on the off-speed stuff and still have the confidence to be able to hit the fastball.

Think about what happens when two cars pass each other on the highway. Let's say that you are traveling in one direction and I'm traveling in the other direction, and we're both going 70 mph. I'm not going to have any idea of how fast you're moving as we pass, nor am I likely to get a clear look at you because I'm only going to see you as a blur of motion.

But if I'm standing still and you're cruising at me at 70 mph, I can see you coming the whole way. As you get closer, I can see every detail of your car. I can judge the speed. I would know when to get out of the way.

The same thing happens with hitting a baseball. If your balance is off—if you move forward instead of going back to initiate your swing—you'll have too much head movement to see the ball clearly and you won't get a good look at the pitch.

Let's get back to the basics: if everything with your mechanics is solid, there's no reason why you won't be able to see the spin or rotation on the ball. But it's still going to take practice, as hitting a breaking ball is one of the toughest things you're going to have to learn. And any pitcher who can throw the curveball and the fastball over for strikes is going to be tough to hit against.

Let's make it even more simple: You have to see the baseball to hit a breaking ball. The breaking ball is tough to hit because it's in the strike zone for only a split second. The fastball is in the strike zone for a longer time so it's easier to adjust, but with a curve or a slider you have a very limited window of opportunity to hit the ball while it's in the strike zone. Now, as you are moving from Point A to Point B with your mechanically sound swing, pop the whip (move back before going forward) to make contact right in that very small window. Bam!—hit that pitch where it's thrown.

But it still goes back to staying strict with the foundation: A slight, smooth head movement; smooth eye movement; you are seeing the ball come to you; your mechanics are square and in a straight line.

I was probably better than most young hitters in adjusting to hitting the breaking ball when I went into pro ball. I didn't have much head movement. I didn't have a long stride. I had a solid foundation of good mechanics.

I credit Rod Carew for showing me the way to build the base that allowed me to hit a good breaking ball. In emulating Rod, I hit with less movement, had a short stride and compact swing, and hit the ball where it was pitched. I wanted to see where the ball was pitched before deciding where to hit it, and that meant being patient enough to wait until the ball reached a certain spot.

Obviously, it helps to have an understanding of the strike zone to become

Another relaxed swing from Rod Carew—it looks like a line drive to left field. Perfect balance and finish, his head and eyes were down on the ball. In emulating Rod, I hit with less movement, had a short stride, and a compact swing.

a complete hitter, a guy who can hit any pitch and use the whole field. I took a lot from Rod's game and it helped to mold me as a player, but I didn't have his speed and had to be true to what I did best.

You may never be Michael Jordan—or Don Mattingly, for that matter. I could do some things well, but I was no Rod Carew. At the end of the day, you have to work hard to get the most out of your unique skills. Be true to yourself and you can't go wrong.

5. Break Out of Slumps.

Whatever happened in the past is gone. You can't let the failure of your last ten at bats have an impact on your next ten at bats.

I define a slump as an extended negative period. In baseball, perhaps you've been hitless for three or four games. In life, it could mean you had a bad haircut, but you have to give it time to grow back. It is just a temporary setback.

Let's say I'm spraying line drives all over the field and none of them are dropping for hits. I'm popping the ball up too much. I'm not seeing the ball well. But that's in the past!

Slumps need to be put in the rearview mirror. Those last ten at bats are gone. They are over. You're never going to get them back. Move ahead to your next game, which is the only thing you can control. You can't be thinking that four days from now, you're going to have to play five games in a row. Focus on the game today. Focus on your next at bat.

It all comes back to keeping things simple. Get a good pitch to hit. Hit a ball hard. Win that individual battle with the pitcher four or five times per day. That's what baseball is all about. Then you string all those individual battles together. If at the end of the year you've had one hundred at bats and you can say you won seventy out of a hundred battles—"I got a good pitch to hit, I hit the ball hard seventy out of a hundred times," then that's pretty impressive.

Say to yourself when you're fighting a slump: "I don't care if I get any hits. I don't care where the ball goes. I'm going to hit the ball hard four times today. And I'm going to take whatever I get from that experience and be positive."

At that point, you can walk away and look in the mirror and can say that you won those battles. Even though you didn't get any hits, you still won those battles. If you keep winning those battles, you will hit .300 someday. The hits will fall, and you'll be successful and consistent.

5

BATTING DRILLS FOR HITTING .300

These drills will help you get the most out of your God-given talent. They are designed to improve your game and to take it to the next level.

—ALEX RODRIGUEZ

Batting drills are a good way to work on getting in a groove to make your swing more consistent. The ultimate goal of any drill is to improve performance and to have the swing be automatic. You program a perfect response, the that swing does exactly what you want it to do once you're playing baseball games. You can't think about mechanics during the game; that mechanically sound swing (chapter 1) must become second nature to you.

The V-grip bat (chapter 3) is perfect for all of these drills, and of course you can use it in games, because with it your hands are automatically in the ideal hitting position. It gives you the freedom to hit different pitches in different locations with that whipping motion of the inside-out swing.

DRILL #1: THE BATTING TEE

A great tool that will teach you what pitches you can handle and what pitches you need to work on, the batting tee allows you to work on every pitch in every location of the strike zone.

Move the tee around to different positions to simulate all the different pitches you'll see in any game. Just keep in mind that the batting tee moves while you keep your feet in the same spot all the time.

Begin with your stance: You put down the tee, get into the batter's box, and mark your feet to know exactly where you are standing. By moving the batting tee you can hit the ball to every part of the field and be able to hit any pitch thrown to any location—outside, middle, middle-in, and inside. To hit the ball in, you have to hit it farther out in front (that's where you would move the tee). And the farther the pitch gets to the outside part of the plate, you now have to hit it farther back (and so that's where the tee moves).

The hardest pitch to hit is the inside pitch, especially since the goal is to hit the ball fair. So that's one of the things you can focus on during your batting tee sessions.

But all of these pitch locations require the same swing. Don't change your swing. Don't change where you step. Everything is exactly the same, except the location of the pitch.

The tee is a valuable tool for honing your swing. (Above and right): Notice that the feet stay in the same position. The ball moves in different locations to change the contact point of the swing. (Below): I'm working on balance: hitting the ball on the inner half of the plate and making sure that I'm balanced as I start the swing. The top three photos and the one at the immediate right all show how I'm working on the ball away and hitting the ball to different areas, and in the bottom three photos I'm working on the ball on the inner half of the plate and making sure I'm in balance.

I'm using the tee drill to keep Sal Fasano's swing short and compact by having him hit the ball the other way.

Coaching Summary

You control your mechanics by marking your feet, putting a line in the dirt to check your stride, and then moving the tee in different directions across the plate. Remember that *you* are moving the tee around; *you* are not moving, and your swing stays the same on all pitch locations. A young hitter needs that continuity and consistency of working on ideal mechanics while adjusting to different pitch locations. Your swing and stride never vary.

Volume: How many swings you take in practice will depend on what you're working on that day. You might want to take ten to twenty swings to make contact with the ball as you face the tee, to hit the left-field; take ten to twenty with tee moved slightly forward, to hit to center-field; and ten to twenty with the tee moved considerably forward, to hit to right field.

In general, the goal is to use the tee to get at least fifty perfect swings, regardless of where you're hitting the ball. That's the way I want you to work: The goal is to work toward perfection of the swing. We are practicing to be perfect.

One-hand tee drills: Some hitters will do one-handed work with the bottom hand. I don't necessarily recommend this for young players, but as you get older and stronger it can be of some value to enhance solid mechanics. I'm not going to ask a ten-year-old to try one-handed drills, though, as he'll end up with some bad habits.

I like this one-leg drill to make sure you are balanced as you begin your shift toward the baseball. The goal is to work toward perfection of the swing. We are practicing to be perfect.

DRILL #2: SOFT TOSS TO THE FRONT

I'll stand about fifteen feet in front of the hitter, about five strides in length, and toss baseballs from different locations. The good thing about soft toss is that the speed is nice and slow—that's beneficial because when we're talking about building the good foundation you'd like to work with a drill that doesn't rush you; no one is going to get hit with the ball; there's no fear of live pitching.

Applications: This drill allows you to watch the stride, see if the hitter is square (using the straight-line, shoulder-width stance). You can simulate pitches to all locations, and troubleshoot any problems and correct mechanics just by asking the hitter to hit balls to certain spots on the field, and to watch what he's doing with his swing.

Soft-toss and a typical Yankee lineup from June 2006:

Johnny Damon (yes)

Derek Jeter (yes)

Alex Rodriguez (yes)

Jason Giambi (no)—but he does use the tee!

Bernie Williams (yes)

Jorge Posada (yes)

Melky Cabrera (yes)

Andy Phillips (yes)

Miguel Cairo (yes)

Sal Fasano (yes)

Craig Wilson (yes)

Gary Sheffield (yes)

Hideki Matsui (yes)

Robinson Cano (yes)

Bobby Abreu (yes)

Soft-toss applications:

- A coach can use soft toss to see if a hitter is striding from Point A to Point B.
- A coach can analyze if a player is getting underneath the ball.
- It's a good way to practice a lot of swings in a controlled atmosphere.
- It's easy to change speeds, and to vary the pace and location of the pitches.

Here, I'm working with Craig Wilson on soft-toss drills at Yankee Stadium. In the photo at left we're doing regular soft toss; in the two bottom photos we're working on one-hand drills. I like soft-tossing the ball to the front because it helps the hitter keep the head square, and as a coach the front-toss drill allows you to keep an eye on a player's stride and swing from the front-on perspective.

Coaching Summary

Soft toss is an effective drill to practice more swings in less time. You can build the foundation of the swing at a slow, relaxed pace that helps to drill muscle-memory and repetition.

Soft-Toss Variations

Variation #1: If a player has a tendency to start his swing by going forward instead of taking a step back, you can have him pick up his foot and do the soft-toss drill while standing on one leg (you can also do this with the batting tee).

This one-leg soft-toss drill develops balance, relaxed hands, and the ability to wait on the pitch while "hanging" with one foot in the air.

Variation #2: From the hanging drill, I'll move to having the hitter use a regular stance. Then I'll go back and forth between the hanging drill and the regular soft-toss drill. The goal is to merge the two drills so the hitter feels comfortable and natural in the stance; the hanging part of it simply adds more balance to it and prevents that forward movement.

Volume: Take forty-five swings (one-half of a bucket) and vary the number of hanging versus regular soft-toss drills.

DRILL #3: SOFT TOSS WITH A SHORT BAT

You can also do the soft-toss drill with what's known as a short bat—37 to 39 ounces and only 30 inches. Tony Clark, who played with the Yankees in 2005, introduced me to this heavy, short bat for drills and it's perfect: In soft toss, with a standard bat, it's easy to hit the ball well, but the short bat makes it more challenging, as you have to wait longer for the ball.

I liked the short bat so much that I created one with the V-handle for my company. The heavy weight of the bat makes you that much more aware if you are pulling off your shoulder, as the weight allows you to *feel* the fact you're pulling around the ball.

Now, if you swing the bat correctly, the weight doesn't feel that heavy. The short bat won't lie to you. It really tells you if you are coming around the ball or hitting underneath it; you have to be more precise with the short bat.

Volume: Ten to twenty perfect swings with the short bat is plenty of work; this is not something I'd recommend to a younger player who is going to struggle with the added weight.

I like soft-toss drills with a short bat (at right in the photo)
because it makes you hit the ball closer to your body.

DRILLS AND CREATIVE THINKING ABOUT HITTING

I've seen coaches experiment with all sorts of different drills to improve their player's ability to hit different pitches:

The Net Drill: The hitter swings the bat at a ball thrown alongside a net; the goal is to not hit the net with the bat—and you won't hit it if you are swinging the bat correctly.

The net drill gives you immediate feedback. You will know right away if you are doing something wrong.

The Chair Drill: I've seen Gerald Perry, the hitting coach of the Oakland A's, do the soft-toss drill by bouncing the ball on the ground to the hitter while he's sitting in a chair. I don't do this particular drill with the Yankees, but the point is that there are many drills that can be effective.

You have to experiment to figure out what's best suited to correct your problems, with constant repetition of the ideal swing.

6

MY ADVICE ON COACHING KIDS

My dad is the most patient coach you'd ever want to meet. He has a very relaxed and kind way of dealing with all the kids in the neighborhood, and he is a great teacher of the game because he loves it so much.

—PRESTON MATTINGLY

Patience is a good place to start when coaching kids in any sport or teaching any skill. Teaching kids is like building a house. You've got to start with a solid foundation from the ground up.

Use the foundation we talked about in chapter 1. Some kids will pick up the fundamental swing right away; other kids may struggle at first so be creative: "Hit me a ground ball." If that's not working: "See if you can hit me a line drive to the second baseman or the shortstop or the third baseman." Have your players try different things in order to perfect the straight stride. Another suggestion: If a player is a right-handed hitter, have him hit the ball down the first-base line to keep him from pulling off the pitch and messing up his stride.

Also realize that if you are coaching young kids:

- It's got to be fun and interesting.
- The best way to teach is through games and drills—see how many balls out of ten pitches your player can hit in one specific spot on the infield.

Coaches must understand that a player, especially a young kid of nine or ten, may not have his coordination developed yet to the point where they can evaluate his ability. That player may have more talent than coaches think, as in one year he may grow four inches and improve his coordination and turn the corner to take his game to the next level.

Don't evaluate a nine-year-old as if he is a teenager, and decide he can't play. That's not fair to the kid and it's a poor way to coach your team. You don't know what's going to happen to the kid's body or when he's going to mature. And so if you can keep giving him the foundation and make it fun and interesting, then when his body changes he may like playing baseball.

The hope is that he will grow up to love playing the game of baseball. Don't beat him up mentally over his struggles; try to make it fun and interesting along the way, or he's going to quit. Otherwise you'll have burned out a kid at ten who might have had a chance to be pretty good.

Good coaching begins with putting everything into perspective and taking a look down the road to understand that this kid may still have some growing up to do.

Even if he's a good player, he still needs to learn how to play the game better. He may be doing well now because he's big and strong for his age, but what if his swing is a wreck?

His success with a bad swing will be short-lived, as when the other kids mature he won't get away with a flawed swing and bad mechanics. The other kids will run right by him, unless you take the time to work on his swing while he's developing as a player.

BASEBALL IS LIFE

I firmly believe that this slogan means you learn a lot of lessons from playing this game the right way. My goal is to help kids learn how to hit and take pride in what they do. I'm not a child psychologist. I raised my kids to learn from competing to win and competing to have fun.

But you can also learn a lot from failure. It hurts to fail, but it also makes you a stronger person. You have two choices when you fail: You can decide to quit playing because it makes you unhappy, or walk down the positive road to realize: "It's okay to fail because it makes me work harder to get better. I'm going to get a hit the next time. I'm going to make the play the next time."

You can learn a lot from failure, but you can also learn a lot from winning. You don't want to boast about winning, and try to intimidate or mock the other team. Learn to have an understanding and an appreciation for what the kids on the other team are feeling. You've been through the pain of the kid hitting the home run off of you, or making the last out of the game and getting taunted by the pitcher who beat you.

What can you learn from failure? Certainly, not to act like that pitcher who made you look bad after you lost. You never want to show up another player and make him feel bad. There's nothing wrong with being happy about winning a baseball game. Be glad that you got the game-winning hit or recorded the final out. But there's never any excuse to make it any more painful for the other team than it is already.

There's a lot to learn from baseball—whether we are winning or losing—from the way we treat other people as we play. That's true of any type of competition, whether it's business, school, or sports.

I've been blessed with success as a player and as a coach with the New York Yankees. I've been able to make a good living from my passion.

You are only as good a hitter as your next at bat.
The foundation you're building in baseball will apply
to anything else you want to pursue in life.

But I can't believe it's any different out there in the "real world." You compete to get a good job. After you get that job, you must compete to do well and move up the ladder to make more money to support your family and provide them with the decent things they deserve. Even within your own company, you will run up against people who don't treat you with respect or who are trying to take your job.

It doesn't matter what the other person does to you. You still have to handle that competitive situation like a decent human being, even if the other guy is handling it the wrong way.

The foundation you're building in baseball—hard work, perseverance, having fun and a passion for success and achievement—will apply to anything else you want to pursue in your life. The choices are up to you to sort out along the way to your future, whether baseball is a part of that future or not.

7

GREAT HITTING MAKES FOR A GREAT GAME

✕

To me he will always be just "Donnie Baseball."

—KIRBY PUCKETT

Kirby Puckett was one of the greatest clutch players of his time. It was hard to find Kirby without a smile on his face.

Kirby Puckett came up with the nickname "Donnie Baseball." I got to know Kirby through the years when we played in the American League together. I got to know him socially at Ken Kaiser's (a MLB umpire) annual charity dinner in Rochester, New York. Kaiser would have a pretty good group of guests, and somehow Kirby and I always hung out together and had a great time. I got to know him more as a person than as just another guy I competed against while he was playing for the Minnesota Twins.

Kirby was not just a great hitter—he was a great player! He exemplified the way you want your kids to play the game. He had fun. He brought a certain

energy and excitement to the field every day. Kirby looked like he was playing Little League baseball, even though he was playing for the Twins in the 1987 World Series. He always had a big smile on his face. He hit the ball all over the field. He was blessed with a great throwing arm, terrific speed for a big man, and he was always making great catches in the outfield. It was impossible not to like the guy. And Kirby was at his best in pressure situations, because he never changed his approach to the game just because everything was on the line.

HITTING IN PRESSURE SITUATIONS

Nothing ever changes with your swing. I was never rattled if the bases were loaded with two outs and the outcome of the game was riding on my at bat. I never changed one single thing about my approach. The guys who hit best with runners in scoring position don't put too much pressure on themselves.

Once again, let's keep it simple: get a good pitch to hit and hit the ball hard. That's about the only thing you can control as a hitter. Swing at a strike and hit the pitch like a bullet. Once you do that, you have won the battle against the pitcher. If you get a good pitch to hit and smash that pitch hard, well, there's not much more you can do to help your team win the game.

You can't control whether you hit a line drive to the shortstop or a bullet right to the center fielder. All you can control is making good contact and looking to hit a quality pitch that you can handle. And it just doesn't matter if the bases are loaded in the ninth inning or the bases are empty in the first inning.

It comes down to a fight between you and the pitcher. Focus on simplifying hitting, and then those pressure situations don't need to be pressure situations. Pressure to perform as a hitter will not help you at any point during the game.

Everything in hitting reverts back to the basics we learned in chapter 1 to build the foundation, and in all the drills in chapter 5 to perfect your swing. The next step is to win the battle with the pitcher every time you go to the plate in every at bat for the entire game. Say you're coming up to the plate in the ninth inning with two men on base and down by two runs. Same darn thing—get a good pitch and hit it hard.

Of course, you want to be the guy who comes through in the clutch. You want to be the guy who can pick up a hit that will tie or win the game. But wanting to be that guy has nothing to do with the daily battle you face against the pitcher. Your personal battle is to defuse the situation of all the noise, and block out what inning it is and all the other useless distractions.

The guy on the mound is in the same situation: he's got more pressure on him because he's the one who has to make a quality to pitch to get you out. Turn it around and put all the pressure on the pitcher—and relax.

Forget about failure. Play the game hard, prepare as best as you can, and accept the reality that baseball is a game that will lead you down the road to failure at certain times. If you don't buy into that reality you'd better wake up and deal with it, because even the greatest players fail a lot over the course of a season, and a career. You can hit a ball dead on the nose and have nothing to show for your effort. The book says you lost because you didn't get a hit with that at bat. But *my* book says you won the battle. The pitcher knows you beat him. The next time he sees you he's going to think, "I got away with murder the last time because he hit a bullet off me." He knows you beat him. Keep playing the game hard, and the hits will fall in bunches.

Kirby was not afraid of making mistakes. He let it all hang out and played the game with freedom. I'm sure he worked his butt off to do all the little things well, but at the end of the day he looked like he was having the time of his life.

Wade Boggs kept his head down and his eyes on the baseball.

Wade Boggs

Boggs would never give away at bats. He was a tough out all the time. But when he came to play for the Yankees, I could see firsthand how hard he was willing to work at his craft.

We'd be down by eight runs or playing at midnight after a two-hour rain delay, and he treated every at bat like a do-or-die situation. He would foul off pitches. He would never swing at bad pitches. His level of concentration was tremendous. And he was consistent with that intense focus for every game of his entire career, and that tells you why he was such a great player.

Another thing I can tell you about Wade is that, when he first came up with the Boston Red Sox, they said he couldn't play third base. But he worked at it for years and turned himself into a very good third baseman. He won a Gold Glove while he was in New York; he worked at his fielding because he would accept nothing less from himself than being the best. He worked long and hard to prove the so-called experts wrong.

Never buy into the negative things other people say about you. You must believe in your ability. Work on getting better every day with your fundamentals and your drills. All the hard work and drills and practice will make you a complete player over time. I want you to develop into a good hitter, but it's also important to be a well-rounded player who can do a lot of things well to help his team win games.

Tony Gwynn

I had the pleasure of playing against Tony in Winter Ball in Puerto Rico in 1983. He was a tremendous hitter. I was playing for Caguas and Tony played for San Juan. He had that effortless swing—sweet, smooth, and easy. In 1984, he won the NL batting title and I won the AL batting title. When I think of Tony, I remember that smooth, mechanically sound swing—he made hitting look so easy.

Chipper Jones of the Atlanta Braves reminds me of Tony, because Chipper also makes hitting look so simple. I'm sure that Tony and Chipper view hitting as a battle. So do I. I always had to work hard to improve my skills, and nothing is ever handed to you in this game. You will have to earn it.

TONY GWYNN: *[Don Mattingly] could hit—whew. When we played together in Puerto Rico, we were the same type of hitter—hit the ball the other way, use the whole field, spray the ball around. Once he got to the big leagues, he developed that power stroke a whole lot quicker*

than I did. I knew from his stroke that he was going to be a good hitter. Donnie had so few strikeouts, and that put him in the mold of a contact hitter: a guy who would go up to the plate just looking to put the bat on the ball. Mattingly was the exception to the norm because he could go up to the plate and put his bat on the ball, but he could also drive it out of the ballpark.

I learned how to hit home runs by talking hitting with Ted Williams. Ted told me in 1992, "As big as you are you should be able to drive the ball out of the ballpark." And then in 1995 I sat down and had a conversation with him, when he said: "Major-league history is made on the ball inside."

He didn't elaborate on that comment, and like most good hitters from the past he didn't feed me the answer; instead, he gave me an idea to think about—and if you're worth your salt as a hitter you will figure it out just based on a fragment of information or a question to consider.

Another line drive from Tony Gwynn; he's on balance as he's coming out of the box. He was one of the greatest players who ever lived.

So when you think about Donnie using his bottom hand to generate power in 1983–'84, that's the same thing that I had to learn in 1995 after hitting for a decade without power. In order to hit the ball out of the park, I had to learn how to use the bottom hand correctly, and to use it efficiently.

Most young hitters don't have the slightest idea of what hitting with the bottom hand means. Here's what I'm talking about: Get into the hitting position. You're in your stance. The pitcher is getting ready to let the ball go. You're in the ready position, which for most guys is taking your hands back and setting your foot down.

Once you get to that point, it's the bottom hand that dominates the swing; it's the bottom hand that allows you to pull the bat though the zone—it gets the bat started in the zone and you generate bat speed by letting the bottom hand become the dominant hand as the bat comes through the zone.

Most young hitters think that you start with the bottom hand, but at some point the top hand takes over the swing—and that's not true. The bottom hand is the dominant hand throughout the swing—and so, once you let your bottom hand do the work, now you can create enough speed that will allow you to drive the ball.

The two players I loved to talk hitting with the most were Don Mattingly and Wade Boggs. Donnie was an example of a hitter who went from just hitting line drives to hitting both home runs and line drives. He went from the guy I was, to the guy who every hitter wants to become—a .300 hitter, a power hitter, and a threat to drive in runs. That's what all hitters dream about. Donnie was able to live that dream of putting it all together.

Whenever the Yankees were on TV, I was sure to keep the game on that channel until after Mattingly hit so I could analyze what he was doing. He had some years that were absolutely unbelievable. His career numbers are almost identical to Kirby Puckett (a Hall of Famer), but because Donnie got injured he doesn't seem to get the credit he deserves. He was the dominant player in the American League from 1984 to '89—there's no doubt about that. His numbers reflect that fact. His back injury slowed him down, but he fought through it as best as he could because he was a tireless worker.

He was a Gold Glove fielder who would hit 30 home runs, drive in 100 runs, score 100 runs, stroke 200 hits. He was not a big guy and yet he was a dominant guy. And a great guy, to be sure.

George Brett was the best clutch hitter I ever played against. Look at the powerful legs, balanced on the bottom and ready to attack.

George Brett

George was one of the most feared hitters of the last fifty years. I never wanted to see him at the plate with the game on the line because he always managed to find a way to drive in those key runs with me on base. You could have a tough lefty pitcher on the mound who retired him on grounders the first two times up, but on the third at bat—and seeing the exact same pitch, George would hit a rifle-shot to the left-field corner to win the game for the Kansas City Royals.

George is another one of those guys who played the game with reckless abandon. He had fun and did everything well—hitting, fielding, and running the bases. He had a great work ethic and was a tremendous competitor.

GEORGE BRETT: *Donnie would take whatever the pitcher would give him and make the most of it. If the pitcher threw a down-and-*

George looks like he's ready to get on top of another high fastball.

away pitch, he's going to get a base hit to left. If they throw it inside, he's going to pull the pitch. He was able to work the whole field. And Charlie Lau, my hitting coach, always told me you're not a real hitter until you can hit the ball all over the place.

Donnie was a great clutch hitter. So many guys who play the game of baseball these days put pressure on themselves late in the game and get very tense at the plate. Donnie was exactly the opposite: He seemed to relax when the game was on the line.

Another thing that made him good is that he always put the ball in play and almost never had any strikeouts. You can hit the ball and move the runner up, and if you strike out you are not moving the runner up—this is where batting average can be a little misleading, because you can make productive outs and they will never show up in the box score.

Donnie didn't draw many walks because if he had one swing per at

bat, he would put the ball in play. A lot of guys foul off four or five pitches and then draw a walk. Donnie had skill to make the most of his swings and convert those swings into doubles and home runs. He would rarely get more than one or two swings per at bat, and he would put them into play because he had good fundamentals and a good swing.

And even though he was a great hitter, he was not unwilling to shorten his swing—if the count did get to two strikes, because there was a pride factor back in the seventies and eighties. You did not want to strike out back then. I used to hate walking back to the dugout with my bat in my hand. I felt like that pitcher beat me. And I hate to get beat up. I had pride in not striking out during my career, and these days the hitters just don't care. You see guys laughing in the dugout after striking out two or three times per game, and that's a disgrace. It is style before substance—they want to look good striking out, and they swing from their ass.

I got along great with Donnie. One year, we were both struggling early in the season in April while the Yankees were in Kansas City. Donnie and I were down around .200 and "Pags" [Mike Pagliarulo] was hitting .180. We were all laughing at each other during batting practice. "I'm swinging worse than you." "No, I'm swinging worse."

After the game we went out for beers—something I would almost never do with opposing players. But I always had a lot of respect for Don and I always had a lot of respect for Pags. We came to the park the next day and, sure enough, Donnie gets a base hit his first time up and I'm laughing my ass off at third base. I doubled in my first at bat and Donnie was laughing his ass off at first base. Then Pags comes up and he strikes out, and we were all laughing at each other.

It was a great thing to go out with my peers while we were all struggling at the same time, talk about what was going through our minds, and

*bragging about how bad we were—and we were three pretty good players
at the time—but we could laugh about our struggles and help each other
out. The game of baseball is meant to be taken seriously, and it's also
something to enjoy with your teammates and friends.*

SET THE GOAL: HIT .300 AND EARN RESPECT

You can't expect to hit .300 unless you love to play baseball. The people who
are the most successful in business and sports are the ones who love what they do
for a living. I'm sure that Bill Gates loves his job—not because of the wealth but
for the fun of competing.

My sister-in-law once said to me about my son Preston, who had a choice
between signing with the Dodgers and playing college baseball at the University
of Tennessee: "If you follow your passion, you will never work a day in your life."

Enjoy playing baseball and have fun as you improve. Don't make learning
how to play the game any more complicated than it has to be. Don't lose your perspective on having fun, because baseball is just a game.

Photo Gallery

Derek Jeter: One of the toughest competitors who has ever played the game.

Jason Giambi: Raw power. The head is down and he's trying to go deep.

Yankee Stadium: Cathedral of the baseball gods.

Johnny Damon: Another guy who always has fun playing the game.

Robinson Cano: He has great mechanics and solid fundamentals, a great young player with huge potential.

Yankee Stadium is the ultimate place to play baseball because there is always a full house.

APPENDIX

*Stats, and Other Mattingly and
New York Yankees Gems*

THE DON MATTINGLY FILE

Donald Arthur Mattingly

Bats: Left

Throws: Left

Born: April 20, 1961, in Evansville, Indiana

Height: 6'

Weight: 185 pounds

Debut: September 8, 1982 vs. Baltimore Orioles

0 AB, 0H, 0HR, 0RBI, 0SB

Final Game: October 1, 1995

Drafted by the New York Yankees in the 19th round of the 1979 amateur
draft.

Minor League Stats

YEAR	TEAM	AGE	LEVEL	G	AB	R	H	2B	3B	HR	RBI	SB	BB	SO	AVG
1979	Oneonta	18	A	53	166	20	58	10	3	3	31	2	30	6	.349
1980	Greensboro	19	A	133	494	92	177	32	5	9	105	8	59	33	.358
1981	Nashville	20	AA	141	547	74	173	35	4	7	98	4	64	55	.316
1982	Columbus	21	AAA	130	476	67	150	24	2	10	75	1	50	24	.315

Source: Baseball-Reference.com

MLB Career Batting Totals

YEAR	AG	TM	LG	G	AB	R	H	2B	3B	HR	RBI	SB	CS	BB	SO	BA	OBP	SLG
1982	21	NYY	AL	7	12	0	2	0	0	0	1	0	0	0	1	.167	.167	.154
1983	22	NYY	AL	91	279	34	79	15	4	4	32	0	0	21	31	.283	.333	.409
1984	23	NYY	AL	153	603	91	207	44	2	23	110	1	1	41	33	.343	.381	.537
1985	24	NYY	AL	159	652	107	211	48	3	35	145	2	2	56	41	.324	.371	.567
1986	25	NYY	AL	162	677	117	238	53	2	31	113	0	0	53	35	.352	.394	.573
1987	26	NYY	AL	141	569	93	186	38	2	30	115	1	4	51	38	.327	.378	.559
1988	27	NYY	AL	144	599	94	186	37	0	18	88	1	0	41	29	.311	.353	.462
1989	28	NYY	AL	158	631	79	191	37	0	23	113	3	0	51	30	.303	.351	.477
1990	29	NYY	AL	102	394	40	101	16	0	5	42	1	0	28	20	.256	.308	.335
1991	30	NYY	AL	152	587	64	169	35	0	9	68	2	0	46	42	.288	.339	.394
1992	31	NYY	AL	157	640	89	184	40	0	14	86	3	0	39	43	.288	.327	.416
1993	32	NYY	AL	134	530	78	154	27	2	17	86	0	0	61	42	.291	.364	.445
1994	33	NYY	AL	97	372	62	113	20	1	6	51	0	0	60	24	.304	.397	.411
1995	34	NYY	AL	128	458	59	132	32	2	7	49	0	2	40	35	.288	.341	.471

14 Seasons

G	AB	R	H	2B	3B	HR	RBI	SB	CS	BB	SO	BA	OBP	SLG
1785	7003	1007	2153	442	20	222	1099	14	9	588	444	.307	.358	.471

162 Game Average

AB	R	H	2B	3B	HR	RBI	SB	CS	BB	SO	BA	OBP	SLG
636	91	195	40	2	20	100	1	1	53	40	.307	.358	.471

Career High

G	AB	R	H	2B	3B	HR	RBI	SB	CS	BB	SO	BA	OBP	SLG
162	677	117	238	53	4	35	145	3	4	61	43	.352	.397	.573

MLB Career Fielding Totals

YEAR	AG	TM	LG	POS	G	PO (putouts)	A (assists)	E	DP (double plays)	FP
1982	21	NYY	AL	OF	6	11	1	0	0	1.000
				1B	1	4	0	0	0	1.000
1983	22	NYY	AL	OF	48	72	3	2	1	.974
				1B	42	278	12	1	30	.997
				2B	1	0	0	0	0	
1984	23	NYY	AL	1B	133	1107	124	5	135	.996
				OF	19	36	2	1	1	.974
1985	24	NYY	AL	1B	159	1318	87	7	154	.995
1986	25	NYY	AL	1B	160	1377	100	6	132	.996
				3B	3	1	11	1	2	.923
				DH	1					

(cont.)

(cont.)

YEAR	AG	TM	LG	POS	G	PO (putouts)	A (assists)	E	DP (double plays)	FP
1987	26	NYY	AL	1B	140	1239	91	5	122	.996
				DH	1					
1988	27	NYY	AL	1B	143	1250	99	9	131	.993
				DH	1					
				OF	1	0	0	0	0	
1989	28	NYY	AL	1B	145	1274	87	7	143	.995
				DH	17					
1990	29	NYY	AL	1B	89	800	78	3	81	.997
				DH	13					
				OF	1	0	0	0	0	
1991	30	NYY	AL	1B	127	1119	77	5	135	.996
				DH	22					
1992	31	NYY	AL	1B	143	1209	116	4	129	.997
				DH	5					
1993	32	NYY	AL	1B	130	1258	84	3	123	.998
				DH	5					
1994	33	NYY	AL	1B	97	919	68	2	95	.998
1995	34	NYY	AL	1B	125	996	81	7	90	.994
Position Total				1B	1634	14148	1104	64	1500	.996
				DH	76	*Games not counted in overall total below*				
				OF	76	121	6	3	2	.977
				3B	3	1	11	1	2	.923
				2B	1	0	0	0	0	
Overall Total					1714	14270	1121	68	1504	.996

The Postseason Batting Line

YEAR	ROUND	TM	OPP	W/L	G	AB	R	H	2B	3B	HR	RBI	BB	SO	BA	OB	SLG
1995	ALDS	NY	SEA	L	5	24	3	10	4	0	1	6	1	5	.41	.440	.708

AL LEADERBOARDS AND AWARDS

ALL-STAR GAMES

1984

1985

1986

1987

1988

1989

AWARDS

1985 Major League Baseball Player of the Year

1985 AL MVP

1993 Lou Gehrig Memorial Award

AL GOLD GLOVES (1B)

1985

1986

1987

1988

1989

1991

1992

1993

1994

SILVER SLUGGERS

1985—AL (1B)

1986—AL (1B)

1987—AL (1B)

AL MVP (TOP 10 IN VOTING)

1984 (5)

1985 (1)

1986 (2)

1987 (7)

BATTING AVERAGE (AL)

1984—.343 (1)

1985—.324 (3)

1986—.352 (2)

1987—.327 (5)

1988—.311 (8)

ON-BASE PERCENTAGE (AL)

1984—.381 (10)

1986—.394 (5)

SLUGGING PERCENTAGE (AL)

1984—.537 (2)

1985—.567 (2)

1986—.573 (1)

1987—.559 (7)

1989—.477 (8)

GAMES (AL)

1986: 162 (2)

1989: 158 (10)

YANKEES RETIRED UNIFORM NUMBERS

BILLY MARTIN

Born: May 16, 1928, in Berkeley, CA

Died: December 25, 1989, in Binghamton, NY

Height: 5' 11"

Weight: 165 pounds

Threw and batted right-handed

Number retired in 1986

BABE RUTH

Born: February 6, 1895, in Baltimore, MD

Died: August 16, 1948, in New York, NY

Height: 6' 2"

Weight: 215 pounds

Threw and batted left-handed

Number retired in 1948

LOU GEHRIG

Born: June 19, 1903, in New York, NY
Died: June 2, 1941, in Riverdale, NY
Height: 6' 1"
Weight: 212 pounds
Threw and batted left-handed
Number retired in 1939

JOE DiMAGGIO

Born: November 25, 1914, in Martinez, CA
Died: March 8, 1999, in Hollywood, FL
Height: 6' 2"
Weight: 193 pounds
Threw and batted right-handed
Number retired in 1952

MICKEY MANTLE

Born: October 20, 1931, in Spavinaw, OK
Died: August 14, 1995, in Dallas, TX
Height: 6'
Weight: 201 pounds
Threw: right and switched hit
Number retired in 1969

YOGI BERRA

Born: May 12, 1925, in St. Louis, MO
Height: 5' 8"
Weight: 191 pounds
Threw and batted right-handed
Number retired in 1972

BILL DICKEY

Born: June 6, 1907, in Bastrop, LA
Died: November 12, 1993, in Little Rock, AR
Height: 6' 1"
Weight: 185 pounds
Threw right-handed and batted left-handed
Number retired in 1972

ROGER MARIS

Born: September 10, 1934, in Hibbing, MN
Died: December 14, 1985, in Houston, TX
Height: 6'
Weight: 197 pounds
Threw right-handed and batted left-handed
Number retired in 1984

PHIL RIZZUTO

Born: September 25, 1917, in New York, NY
Height: 5' 6"
Weight: 150 pounds
Threw and batted right-handed
Number retired in 1985

THURMAN MUNSON

Born: June 7, 1947, in Akron, OH
Died: August 2, 1979, in Canton, OH
Height: 5' 11"
Weight: 190 pounds
Threw and batted right-handed
Number retired in 1979

WHITEY FORD

Born: October 21, 1928, in New York, NY
Height: 5' 10"
Weight: 181 pounds
Threw and batted left-handed
Number retired in 1974

DONALD ARTHUR MATTINGLY

Born: April 20, 1961, in Evansville, IN
Height: 6'
Weight: 185 pounds
Threw and batted left-handed
Number retired in 1997

ELSTON HOWARD

Born: February 23, 1929, in St. Louis, MO
Died: December 14, 1980, in New York, NY
Height: 6' 2"
Weight: 196 pounds
Threw and batted right-handed
Number retired in 1984

CASEY STENGEL

Born: July 30, 1889, in Kansas City, MO
Died: September 29, 1975, in Glendale, CA
Height: 5' 11"
Weight: 175 pounds
Threw and batted left-handed
Number retired in 1979

REGGIE JACKSON

Born: May 18, 1946, in Wyncote, PA
Height: 5' 10"
Weight: 181 pounds
Threw and batted left-handed
Number retired in 1993

RON GUIDRY

Born: August 28, 1950, in Lafayette, LA
Height: 5' 11"
Weight: 165 pounds
Threw and batted left-handed
Number retired in 2003
Source: New York Yankees

Major League Baseball Leaders

(Note: Based on 1,000 career games played and at bats. Boldface denotes active players.)

Batting Average

All-Time Leaders
"Top 100"

NAME	BATTING AVERAGE	RANK
Ty Cobb	.366 (.36636)	1
Rogers Hornsby	.358 (.35850)	2
Joe Jackson	.356 (.35575)	3
Pete Browning	.349 (.34892)	4
Ed Delahanty	.346 (.34590)	5
Tris Speaker	.345 (.34468)	6
Ted Williams	.344 (.34441)	7
Billy Hamilton	.344 (.34429)	8
Dan Brouthers	.342 (.34213)	9
Babe Ruth	.342 (.34207)	10
Harry Heilmann	.342(.34159)	11
Willie Keeler	.341 (.34129)	12
Bill Terry	.341 (.34116)	13
George Sisler	.340 (.34015)	14
Lou Gehrig	.340 (.34008)	15
Jesse Burkett	.338 (.33844)	16
Tony Gwynn	.338 (.33818)	17

(cont.)

(cont.)

Nap Lajoie	.338 (.33810)	18
Riggs Stephenson	.336 (.33607)	19
Al Simmons	.334 (.33417)	20
John McGraw	.334 (.33359)	21
Tip O'Neill	.334 (.33357)	22
Paul Waner	.333 (.33323)	23
Eddie Collins	.333 (.33320)	24
Todd Helton	.333 (.33294)	25
Mike Donlin	.333 (.33264)	26
Stan Musial	.331 (.33084)	27
Sam Thompson	.331 (.33072)	28
Heinie Manush	.330 (.32976)	29
Cap Anson	.329 (.32909)	30
Wade Boggs	.328 (.32789)	31
Rod Carew	.328 (.32775)	32
Honus Wagner	.327 (.32742)	33
Bob Fothergill	.325 (.32548)	34
Jimmie Foxx	.325 (.32530)	35
Earle Combs	.325 (.32475)	36
Vladimir Guerrero	.325 (.32461)	37
Joe DiMaggio	.325 (.32459)	38
Babe Herman	.324 (.32447)	39

Hugh Duffy	.324 (.32406)	40
Joe Medwick	.324 (.32364)	41
Edd Roush	.323 (.32269)	42
Sam Rice	.322 (.32226)	43
Ross Youngs	.322 (.32224)	44
Kiki Cuyler	.321 (.32105)	45
Charlie Gehringer	.320 (.32043)	46
Chuck Klein	.320 (.32007)	47
Pie Traynor	.320 (.31962)	48
Mickey Cochrane	.320 (.31960)	49
Ken Williams	.319 (.31921)	50
Nomar Garciaparra	.318 (.31809)	51
Kirby Puckett	.318 (.31806)	52
Denny Lyons	.318 (.31790)	53
Earl Averill	.318 (.31780)	54
Arky Vaughan	.318 (.31758)	55
Roberto Clemente	.317 (.31733)	56
Chick Hafey	.317 (.31697)	57
Joe Kelley	.317 (.31687)	58
Zack Wheat	.317 (.31671)	59
Derek Jeter	.317 (.31664)	60
Roger Connor	.317 (.31653)	61

(cont.)

(cont.)

Lloyd Waner	.316 (.31639)	62
Frankie Frisch	.316 (.31607)	63
Goose Goslin	.316 (.31597)	64
George Van Haltren	.316 (.31567)	65
Bibb Falk	.314 (.31449)	66
Manny Ramirez	.314 (.31422)	67
Cecil Travis	.314 (.31420)	68
Hank Greenberg	.313 (.31350)	69
Jack Fournier	.313 (.31317)	70
Elmer Flick	.313 (.31303)	71
Larry Walker	.313 (.31273)	72
Bill Dickey	.313 (.31254)	73
Dale Mitchell	.312 (.31225)	74
Johnny Mize	.312 (.31212)	75
Joe Sewell	.312 (.31211)	76
Elmer Smith	.312 (.31203)	77
Fred Clarke	.312 (.31186)	78
Barney McCosky	.312 (.31184)	79
Edgar Martinez	.312 (.31152)	80
Hughie Jennings	.311 (.31138)	81
Freddie Lindstrom	.311 (.31135)	82
Bing Miller	.311 (.31133)	83

Jackie Robinson	.311 (.31126)	84
Baby Doll Jacobson	.311 (.31124)	85
Taffy Wright	.311 (.31119)	86
Rip Radchiff	.311 (.31100)	87
Ginger Beaumont	.311 (.31078)	88
Mike Tiernan	.311 (.31053)	89
Luke Appling	.310 (.31041)	90
Irish Meusel	.310 (.31041)	91
Bobby Veach	.310 (.30995)	92
Henry Larkin	.310 (.30990)	93
Jim O'Rourke	.310 (.30989)	94
Jim Bottomley	.310 (.30960)	95
John Stone	.310 (.30952)	96
Sam Crawford	.309 (.30940)	97
Mike Piazza	.309 (.30930)	98
Bob Meusel	.309 (.30922)	99
Oyster Burns	.309 (.30894)	100

Hits

All-Time Leaders
"Top 100"

NAME	HITS	RANK
Pete Rose	4,256	1
Ty Cobb	4,189	2
Hank Aaron	3,771	3
Stan Musial	3,630	4
Tris Speaker	3,514	5
Carl Yastrzemski	3,419	6
Honus Wagner	3,415	7
Paul Molitor	3,319	8
Eddie Collins	3,315	9
Willie Mays	3,283	10
Eddie Murray	3,255	11
Nap Lajoie	3,242	12
Cal Ripken, Jr.	3,184	13
George Brett	3,154	14
Paul Waner	3,152	15
Robin Yount	3,142	16
Tony Gwynn	3,141	17
Dave Winfield	3,110	18

Rickey Henderson	3,055	19
Rod Carew	3,053	20
Lou Brock	3,023	21
Rafael Palmeiro	3,020	22
Wade Boggs	3,010	23
Al Kaline	3,007	24
Roberto Clemente	3,000	25
Cap Anson	2,995	26
Sam Rice	2,987	27
Sam Crawford	2,961	28
Frank Robinson	2,943	29
Willie Keeler	2,932	30
Jake Beckley	2,930	31
Craig Biggio	2,930	32
Rogers Hornsby	2,930	33
Al Simmons	2,927	34
Zack Wheat	2,884	35
Frankie Frisch	2,880	36
Mel Ott	2,876	37
Babe Ruth	2,873	38
Harold Baines	2,866	39
Jesse Burkett	2,850	40

(cont.)

(cont.)

Brooks Robinson	2,848	41
Barry Bonds	2,841	42
Charlie Gehringer	2,839	43
George Sisler	2,812	44
Andre Dawson	2,774	45
Vada Pinson	2,757	46
Luke Appling	2,749	47
Al Oliver	2,743	48
Goose Goslin	2,735	49
Tony Perez	2,732	50
Roberto Alomar	2,724	51
Lou Gehrig	2,721	52
Rusty Staub	2,716	53
Bill Buckner	2,715	54
Dave Parker	2,712	55
Billy Williams	2,711	56
Doc Cramer	2,705	57
Luis Aparicio	2,677	58
Fred Clarke	2,672	59
Max Carey	2,665	60
Nellie Fox	2,663	61
Lave Cross	2,660	62

George Davis	2,660	63
Harry Heilmann	2,660	64
Ted Williams	2,654	65
Jimmie Foxx	2,646	66
Rabbit Maranville	2,605	67
Tim Raines	2,605	68
Steve Garvey	2,599	69
Ed Delahanty	2,596	70
Reggie Jackson	2,584	71
Ernie Banks	2,583	72
Richie Ashburn	2,574	73
Julio Franco	2,566	74
Willie Davis	2,561	75
George Van Haltren	2,532	76
Steve Finley	2,531	77
Heinie Manush	2,524	78
Joe Morgan	2,517	79
Buddy Bell	2,514	80
Jimmy Ryan	2,502	81
Mickey Vernon	2,495	82
Fred McGriff	2,490	83
Ted Simmons	2,472	84

(cont.)

(cont.)

Omar Vizquel	2,472	85
Joe Medwick	2,471	86
Roger Connor	2,467	87
Harry Hooper	2,466	88
Ozzie Smith	2,460	89
Lloyd Waner	2,459	90
Bill Dahlen	2,457	91
Jim Rice	2,452	92
Red Schoendienst	2,449	93
Dwight Evans	2,446	94
Mark Grace	2,445	95
Pie Traynor	2,416	96
Mickey Mantle	2,415	97
Ken Griffey, Jr.	2,412	98
Stuffy McInnis	2,405	99
Gary Sheffield	2,390	100

Doubles

All-Time Leaders
"Top 100"

NAME	DOUBLES	RANK
Tris Speaker	792	1
Pete Rose	746	2
Stan Musial	725	3
Ty Cobb	724	4
George Brett	665	5
Nap Lajoie	657	6
Carl Yastrzemski	646	7
Honus Wagner	640	8
Craig Biggio	637	9
Hank Aaron	624	10
Paul Molitor	605	11
Paul Waner	605	12
Cal Ripken, Jr.	603	13
Barry Bonds	587	14
Rafael Palmeiro	585	15
Robin Yount	583	16
Wade Boggs	578	17
Charlie Gehringer	574	18

(cont.)

(cont.)

Eddie Murray	560	19
Luis Gonzalez	547	20
Tony Gwynn	543	21
Harry Heilmann	542	22
Rogers Hornsby	541	23
Joe Medwick	540	24
Dave Winfield	540	25
Al Simmons	539	26
Lou Gehrig	534	27
Al Oliver	529	28
Cap Anson	528	29
Frank Robinson	528	30
Dave Parker	526	31
Ted Williams	525	32
Willie Mays	523	33
Ed Delahanty	522	34
Joe Cronin	515	35
Edgar Martinez	514	36
Mark Grace	511	37
Rickey Henderson	510	38
Babe Ruth	506	39
Tony Perez	505	40

Roberto Alomar	504	41
Andre Dawson	503	42
Jeff Kent	501	43
Goose Goslin	500	44
John Olerud	500	45
Rusty Staub	499	46
Bill Buckner	498	47
Al Kaline	498	48
Sam Rice	498	49
Heinie Manush	491	50
Mickey Vernon	490	51
Jeff Bagwell	488	52
Harold Baines	488	53
Mel Ott	488	54
Lou Brock	486	55
Billy Herman	486	56
Vada Pinson	485	57
Hal McRae	484	58
Dwight Evans	483	59
Ted Simmons	483	60
Brooks Robinson	482	61
Zack Wheat	476	62

(cont.)

(cont.)

Jake Beckley	473	63
Ivan Rodriguez	473	64
Larry Walker	471	65
Frankie Frisch	466	66
Jim Bottomley	465	67
Reggie Jackson	463	68
Dan Brouthers	460	69
Sam Crawford	458	70
Jimmie Foxx	458	71
Frank Thomas	458	72
Jimmy Dykes	453	73
George Davis	451	74
Paul O'Neill	451	75
Jimmy Ryan	451	76
Ken Griffey, Jr.	449	77
Joe Morgan	449	78
Bernie Williams	449	79
Steve Finley	446	80
Rod Carew	445	81
George Burns	444	82
Andres Galarraga	444	83
Gary Gaetti	443	84

Dick Bartell	442	85
Don Mattingly	442	86
Roger Connor	441	87
Barry Larkin	441	88
Fred McGriff	441	89
Luke Appling	440	90
Will Clark	440	91
Roberto Clemente	440	92
Steve Garvey	440	93
B. J. Surhoff	440	94
Eddie Collins	438	95
Manny Ramirez	438	96
Cesar Cedeno	436	97
Joe Sewell	436	98
Wally Moses	435	99
Billy Williams	434	100

Triples

All-Time Leaders
"Top 100"

NAME	TRIPLES	RANK
Sam Crawford	309	1
Ty Cobb	295	2
Honus Wagner	252	3
Jake Beckley	243	4
Roger Connor	233	5
Tris Speaker	222	6
Fred Clarke	220	7
Dan Brouthers	205	8
Joe Kelley	194	9
Paul Waner	191	10
Bid McPhee	188	11
Eddie Collins	187	12
Ed Delahanty	185	13
Sam Rice	184	14
Jesse Burkett	182	15
Edd Roush	182	16
Ed Konetchy	181	17
Buck Ewing	178	18

Rabbit Maranville	177	19
Stan Musial	177	20
Harry Stovey	174	21
Goose Goslin	173	22
Tommy Leach	172	23
Zack Wheat	172	24
Rogers Hornsby	169	25
Joe Jackson	168	26
Roberto Clemente	166	27
Sherry Magee	166	28
Jake Daubert	165	29
Elmer Flick	164	30
George Sisler	164	31
Pie Traynor	164	32
Bill Dahlen	163	33
George Davis	163	34
Lou Gehrig	163	35
Nap Lajoie	163	36
Mike Tiernan	162	37
George Van Haltren	161	38
Harry Hooper	160	39
Heinie Manush	160	40

(cont.)

(cont.)

Sam Thompson	160	41
Max Carey	159	42
Joe Judge	159	43
Ed McKean	158	44
Kiki Cuyler	157	45
Jimmy Ryan	157	46
Tommy Corcoran	155	47
Earle Combs	154	48
Jim Bottomley	151	49
Harry Heilmann	151	50
Kip Selbach	149	51
Al Simmons	149	52
Wally Pipp	148	53
Enos Slaughter	148	54
Bobby Veach	147	55
Willie Wilson	147	56
Charlie Gehringer	146	57
Harry Davis	145	58
Willie Keeler	145	59
Bobby Wallace	143	60
Lou Brock	141	61
Willie Mays	140	62

John Reilly	139	63
Tom Brown	138	64
Willie Davis	138	65
Frankie Frisch	138	66
Jimmy Williams	138	67
George Brett	137	68
Babe Ruth	136	69
Jimmy Sheckard	136	70
Elmer Smith	136	71
Lave Cross	135	72
Pete Rose	135	73
Shano Collins	133	74
Jim O'Rourke	132	75
George Wood	132	76
Brett Butler	131	77
Joe DiMaggio	131	78
Buck Freeman	131	79
Buddy Myer	130	80
Oyster Burns	129	81
Larry Gardner	129	82
Earl Averill	128	83
Arky Vaughan	128	84

(cont.)

(cont.)

Vada Pinson	127	85
Hardy Richardson	126	86
Robin Yount	126	87
Jimmie Foxx	125	88
John Anderson	124	89
Cap Anson	124	90
Hal Chase	124	91
Steve Finley	124	92
Frank Schulte	124	93
Larry Doyle	123	94
Duke Farrell	123	95
Dummy Hoy	121	96
Mickey Vernon	120	97
Hugh Duffy	119	98
Fred Pfeffer	119	99
Joe Cronin	118	100

Home Runs

All-Time Leaders
"Top 100"

NAME	HOME RUNS	RANK
Hank Aaron	755	1
Barry Bonds	734	2
Babe Ruth	714	3
Willie Mays	660	4
Sammy Sosa	588	5
Frank Robinson	586	6
Mark McGwire	583	7
Harmon Killebrew	573	8
Rafael Palmeiro	569	9
Ken Griffey, Jr.	563	10
Reggie Jackson	563	11
Mike Schmidt	548	12
Mickey Mantle	536	13
Jimmie Foxx	534	14
Willie McCovey	521	15
Ted Williams	521	16
Ernie Banks	512	17
Eddie Mathews	512	18

(cont.)

(cont.)

Mel Ott	511	19
Eddie Murray	504	20
Lou Gehrig	493	21
Fred McGriff	493	22
Frank Thomas	487	23
Stan Musial	475	24
Willie Stargell	475	25
Jim Thome	472	26
Manny Ramirez	470	27
Dave Winfield	465	28
Alex Rodriguez	464	29
Jose Canseco	462	30
Gary Sheffield	455	31
Carl Yastrzemski	452	32
Jeff Bagwell	449	33
Dave Kingman	442	34
Andre Dawson	438	35
Juan Gonzalez	434	36
Cal Ripken, Jr.	431	37
Billy Williams	426	38
Mike Piazza	419	39
Darrell Evans	414	40

Carlos Delgado		407	41
Duke Snider		407	42
Andres Galarraga		399	43
Al Kaline		399	44
Dale Murphy		398	45
Joe Carter		396	46
Graig Nettles		390	47
Johnny Bench		389	48
Dwight Evans		385	49
Harold Baines		384	50
Larry Walker		383	51
Frank Howard		382	52
Jim Rice		382	53
Albert Belle		381	54
Orlando Cepeda		379	55
Tony Perez		379	56
Matt Williams		378	57
Norm Cash		377	58
Carlton Fisk		376	59
Rocky Colavito		374	60
Gil Hodges		370	61
Ralph Kiner		369	62

(cont.)

(cont.)

Joe DiMaggio	361	63
Gary Gaetti	360	64
Johnny Mize	359	65
Yogi Berra	358	66
Chipper Jones	357	67
Greg Vaughn	355	68
Lee May	354	69
Ellis Burks	352	70
Dick Allen	351	71
Chili Davis	350	72
Jim Edmonds	350	73
Jason Giambi	350	74
George Foster	348	75
Jeff Kent	345	76
Andruw Jones	342	77
Ron Santo	342	75
Jack Clark	340	79
Tino Martinez	339	80
Dave Parker	339	81
Boog Powell	339	82
Don Baylor	338	83
Vladimir Guerrero	338	84

Joe Adcock	336	85
Darryl Strawberry	335	86
Bobby Bonds	332	87
Luis Gonzalez	331	88
Hank Greenberg	331	89
Mo Vaughn	328	90
Willie Horton	325	91
Gary Carter	324	92
Lance Parrish	324	93
Ron Gant	321	94
Vinny Castilla	320	95
Moises Alou	319	96
Cecil Fielder	319	97
Shawn Green	318	98
Roy Sievers	318	99
George Brett	317	100

Runs Batted In

All-Time Leaders
"Top 100"

NAME	RBI	RANK
Hank Aaron	2,297	1
Babe Ruth	2,213	2
Lou Gehrig	1,995	3
Stan Musial	1,951	4
Ty Cobb	1,937	5
Barry Bonds	1,930	6
Jimmie Foxx	1,922	7
Eddie Murray	1,917	8
Willie Mays	1,903	9
Cap Anson	1,879	10
Mel Ott	1,860	11
Carl Yastrzemski	1,844	12
Ted Williams	1,839	13
Rafael Palmeiro	1,835	14
Dave Winfield	1,833	15
Al Simmons	1,827	16
Frank Robinson	1,812	17
Honus Wagner	1,732	18

Reggie Jackson	1,702	19
Cal Ripken, Jr.	1,695	20
Tony Perez	1,652	21
Ernie Banks	1,636	22
Harold Baines	1,628	23
Goose Goslin	1,609	24
Ken Griffey, Jr.	1,608	25
Nap Lajoie	1,599	26
George Brett	1,595	27
Mike Schmidt	1,595	28
Andre Dawson	1,591	29
Rogers Hornsby	1,584	30
Harmon Killebrew	1,584	31
Al Kaline	1,583	32
Frank Thomas	1,579	33
Jake Beckley	1,575	34
Sammy Sosa	1,575	35
Willie McCovey	1,555	36
Fred McGriff	1,550	37
Willie Stargell	1,540	38
Harry Heilmann	1,539	39
Joe DiMaggio	1,537	40

(cont.)

(cont.)

Jeff Bagwell	1,529	41
Tris Speaker	1,529	42
Sam Crawford	1,525	43
Manny Ramirez	1,516	44
Mickey Mantle	1,509	45
Gary Sheffield	1,501	46
Dave Parker	1,493	47
Billy Williams	1,475	48
Rusty Staub	1,466	49
Ed Delahanty	1,464	50
Eddie Mathews	1,453	51
Jim Rice	1,451	52
Joe Carter	1,445	53
George Davis	1,437	54
Yogi Berra	1,430	55
Charlie Gehringer	1,427	56
Andres Galarraga	1,425	57
Joe Cronin	1,424	58
Jim Bottomley	1,422	59
Mark McGwire	1,414	60
Jose Canseco	1,407	61
Robin Yount	1,406	62

Juan Gonzalez	1,404	63
Ted Simmons	1,389	64
Dwight Evans	1,384	65
Joe Medwick	1,383	66
Jeff Kent	1,380	67
Johnny Bench	1,376	68
Chili Davis	1,372	69
Lave Cross	1,371	70
Orlando Cepeda	1,365	71
Brooks Robinson	1,357	72
Darrell Evans	1,354	73
Alex Rodriguez	1,347	74
Gary Gaetti	1,341	75
Johnny Mize	1,337	76
Duke Snider	1,333	77
Ron Santo	1,331	78
Carlton Fisk	1,330	79
Al Oliver	1,326	80
Luis Gonzalez	1,324	81
Roger Connor	1,322	82
Ruben Sierra	1,322	83
Graig Nettles	1,314	84

(cont.)

(cont.)

Pete Rose	1,314	85
Mickey Vernon	1,311	86
Larry Walker	1,311	87
Paul Waner	1,309	88
Steve Garvey	1,308	89
Paul Molitor	1,307	90
Roberto Clemente	1,305	91
Enos Slaughter	1,304	92
Hugh Duffy	1,302	93
Jim Thome	1,302	94
Eddie Collins	1,300	95
Sam Thompson	1,299	96
Dan Brouthers	1,296	97
Mike Piazza	1,291	98
Carlos Delgado	1,287	99
Del Ennis	1,284	100

Runs Scored

All-Time Leaders
"Top 100"

NAME	RUNS	RANK
Rickey Henderson	2,295	1
Ty Cobb	2,246	2
Hank Aaron	2,174	3
Babe Ruth	2,174	4
Pete Rose	2,165	5
Barry Bonds	2,152	6
Willie Mays	2,062	7
Stan Musial	1,949	8
Lou Gehrig	1,888	9
Tris Speaker	1,882	10
Mel Ott	1,859	11
Frank Robinson	1,829	12
Eddie Collins	1,821	13
Carl Yastrzemski	1,816	14
Ted Williams	1,798	15
Paul Molitor	1,782	16
Craig Biggio	1,776	17
Charlie Gehringer	1,774	18

(cont.)

(cont.)

Jimmie Foxx	1,751	19
Honus Wagner	1,736	20
Jesse Burkett	1,720	21
Cap Anson	1,719	22
Willie Keeler	1,719	23
Billy Hamilton	1,690	24
Bid McPhee	1,678	25
Mickey Mantle	1,677	26
Dave Winfield	1,669	27
Rafael Palmeiro	1,663	28
Joe Morgan	1,650	29
Cal Ripken, Jr.	1,647	30
Jimmy Ryan	1,642	31
George Van Haltren	1,639	32
Robin Yount	1,632	33
Eddie Murray	1,627	34
Paul Waner	1,627	35
Al Kaline	1,622	36
Roger Connor	1,620	37
Fred Clarke	1,619	38
Lou Brock	1,610	39
Jake Beckley	1,600	40

Ed Delahanty	1,599	41
Bill Dahlen	1,589	42
George Brett	1,583	43
Rogers Hornsby	1,579	44
Tim Raines	1,571	45
Hugh Duffy	1,552	46
Reggie Jackson	1,551	47
Max Carey	1,545	48
George Davis	1,539	49
Frankie Frisch	1,532	50
Dan Brouthers	1,523	51
Tom Brown	1,521	52
Jeff Bagwell	1,517	53
Sam Rice	1,514	54
Wade Boggs	1,513	55
Eddie Mathews	1,509	56
Roberto Alomar	1,508	57
Al Simmons	1,507	58
Mike Schmidt	1,506	59
Nap Lajoie	1,504	60
Harry Stovey	1,492	61
Goose Goslin	1,483	62

(cont.)

(cont.)

Arlie Latham	1,478	63
Dwight Evans	1,470	64
Ken Griffey, Jr.	1,467	65
Herman Long	1,455	66
Jim O'Rourke	1,446	67
Kenny Lofton	1,442	68
Steve Finley	1,434	69
Gary Sheffield	1,433	70
Harry Hooper	1,429	71
Rod Carew	1,424	72
Dummy Hoy	1,424	73
Sammy Sosa	1,422	74
Joe Kelley	1,421	75
Roberto Clemente	1,416	76
Billy Williams	1,410	77
John Ward	1,408	78
Mike Griffin	1,405	79
Frank Thomas	1,404	80
Sam Crawford	1,391	81
Joe DiMaggio	1,390	82
Lou Whitaker	1,386	83
Tony Gwynn	1,383	84

Andre Dawson	1,373	85
Vada Pinson	1,366	86
Bernie Williams	1,366	87
Brett Butler	1,359	88
Alex Rodriguez	1,358	89
Doc Cramer	1,357	90
King Kelly	1,357	91
Tommy Leach	1,355	92
Larry Walker	1,355	93
Fred McGriff	1,349	94
Darrell Evans	1,344	95
Pee Wee Reese	1,338	96
Luis Aparicio	1,335	97
Lave Cross	1,333	98
Barry Larkin	1,329	99
George Gore	1,327	100

Slugging Average
All-Time Leaders
"Top 100"

NAME	SLUGGING AVERAGE	RANK
Babe Ruth	.690 (.68973)	1
Ted Williams	.634 (.63379)	2
Lou Gehrig	.632 (.63242)	3
Jimmie Foxx	.609 (.60929)	4
Barry Bonds	.608 (.60839)	5
Hank Greenberg	.605 (.60505)	6
Manny Ramirez	600 (.60015)	7
Todd Helton	.593 (.59322)	8
Mark McGwire	.588 (.58817)	9
Vladimir Guerrero	.583 (.58270)	10
Joe DiMaggio	.579 (.57880)	11
Rogers Hornsby	.577 (.57653)	12
Alex Rodriguez	.573 (.57263)	13
Lance Berkman	.567 (.56659)	14
Frank Thomas	.566 (.56629)	15
Larry Walker	.565 (.56522)	16
Jim Thome	.565 (.56483)	17
Albert Belle	.564 (.56381)	18

Johnny Mize	.562 (.56201)	19
Juan Gonzalez	.561 (.56071)	20
Stan Musial	.559 (.55906)	21
Carlos Delgado	.558 (.55774)	22
Willie Mays	.557 (.55749)	23
Ken Griffey, Jr.	.557 (.55700)	24
Mickey Mantle	.557 (.55678)	25
Hank Aaron	.555 (.55451)	26
Mike Piazza	.551 (.55135)	27
David Ortiz	.550 (.54965)	28
Ralph Kiner	.548 (.54793)	29
Hack Wilson	.545 (.54475)	30
Chuck Klein	.543 (.54302)	31
Chipper Jones	.542 (.54158)	32
Jason Giambi	.541 (.54093)	33
Jeff Bagwell	.540 (.54034)	34
Nomar Garciaparra	.540 (.54015)	35
Duke Snider	.540 (.53973)	36
Jim Edmonds	.539 (.53851)	37
Frank Robinson	.537 (.53698)	38
Sammy Sosa	.537 (.53696)	39
Al Simmons	.535 (.53488)	40

(cont.)

(cont.)

Dick Allen	.534 (.53364)	41
Earl Averill	.534 (.53361)	42
Mel Ott	.533 (.53310)	43
Babe Herman	.532 (.53186)	44
Ken Williams	.530 (.53044)	45
Willie Stargell	.529 (.52857)	46
Mike Schmidt	.527 (.52730)	47
Richie Sexson	.526 (.52634)	48
Chick Hafey	.526 (.52605)	49
Gary Sheffield	.525 (.52520)	50
Brian Giles	.525 (.52510)	51
Mo Vaughn	.523 (.52314)	52
Hal Trosky	.522 (.52160)	53
Wally Berger	.522 (.52160)	54
Harry Heilmann	.520 (.52048)	55
Kevin Mitchell	.520 (.51984)	56
Dan Brouthers	.519 (.51915)	57
Charlie Keller	.518 (.51768)	58
Joe Jackson	.517 (.51737)	59
Moises Alou	.516 (.51622)	60
Edgar Martinez	.515 (.51546)	61
Scott Rolen	.515 (.51488)	62

Willie McCovey	.515 (.51470)	63
Jose Canseco	.515 (.51452)	64
Rafael Palmeiro	.515 (.51451)	65
Magglio Ordonez	.513 (.51307)	66
Ty Cobb	.512 (.51198)	67
Ellis Burks	.510 (.51037)	68
Eddie Mathews	.509 (.50943)	69
Fred McGriff	.509 (.50908)	70
Jeff Heath	.509 (.50881)	71
Harmon Killebrew	.509 (.50853)	72
Ryan Klesko	.507 (.50714)	73
Bobby Abreu	.507 (.50663)	74
Bob Johnson	.506 (.50592)	75
Bill Terry	.506 (.50591)	76
Darryl Strawberry	.505 (.50535)	77
Andruw Jones	.505 (.50531)	78
Ed Delahanty	.505 (.50513)	79
Sam Thompson	.505 (.50468)	80
Joe Medwick	.505 (.50452)	81
Jeff Kent	.504 (.50436)	82
Troy Glaus	.503 (.50272)	83
Jim Rice	.502 (.50201)	84

(cont.)

(cont.)

Tris Speaker	.500 (.50034)	85
David Justice	.500 (.50027)	86
Jim Bottomley	.500 (.50020)	87
Derrek Lee	.500 (.50000)	88
Goose Goslin	.500 (.49965)	89
Roy Campanella	.500 (.49964)	90
Ernie Banks	.500 (.49952)	91
Orlando Cepeda	.499 (.49943)	92
Bob Horner	.499 (.49934)	93
Geoff Jenkins	.499 (.49912)	94
Dante Bichette	.499 (.49882)	95
Shawn Green	.499 (.49879)	96
Andres Galarraga	.499 (.49876)	97
Frank Howard	.499 (.49861)	98
Tim Salmon	.498 (.49848)	99
Ted Kluszewski	.498 (.49772)	100

On-Base Percentage

All-Time Leaders
"Top 100"

NAME	OBP (RAW)	RANK
Ted Williams	.482 (.4817)	1
Babe Ruth	.474 (.4739)	2
John McGraw	.466 (.4655)	3
Billy Hamilton	.455 (.4552)	4
Lou Gehrig	.447 (.4474)	5
Barry Bonds	.443 (.4429)	6
Rogers Hornsby	.434 (.4337)	7
Ty Cobb	.433 (.4330)	8
Todd Helton	.430 (.4300)	9
Jimmie Foxx	.428 (.4283)	10
Tris Speaker	.428 (.4279)	11
Eddie Collins	.424 (.4244)	12
Frank Thomas	.424 (.4242)	13
Ferris Fain	.424 (.4241)	14
Dan Brouthers	.423 (.4233)	15
Max Bishop	.423 (.4227)	16
Joe Jackson	.423 (.4227)	17
Mickey Mantle	.421 (.4205)	18

(cont.)

(cont.)

Mickey Cochrane	.419 (.4192)	19
Edgar Martinez	.418 (.4178)	20
Stan Musial	.417 (.4167)	21
Lance Berkman	.416 (.4161)	22
Cupid Childs	.416 (.4158)	23
Jesse Burkett	.415 (.4151)	24
Wade Boggs	.415 (.4150)	25
Mel Ott	.414 (.4140)	26
Roy Thomas	.413 (.4135)	27
Jason Giambi	.413 (.4134)	28
Denny Lyons	.413 (.4130)	29
Bobby Abreu	.412 (.4124)	30
Hank Greenberg	.412 (.4118)	31
Ed Delahanty	.411 (.4114)	32
Manny Ramirez	.411 (.4110)	33
Charlie Keller	.410 (.4099)	34
Eddie Stanky	.410 (.4098)	35
Harry Heilmann	.409 (.4095)	36
Pete Browning	.409 (.4089)	37
Jackie Robinson	.409 (.4089)	38
Jim Thome	.409 (.4089)	39
Brian Giles	.408 (.4083)	40

Roy Cullenbine	.408 (.4082)	41
Jeff Bagwell	.408 (.4076)	42
Riggs Stephenson	.406 (.4065)	43
Arky Vaughan	.406 (.4058)	44
Paul Waner	.404 (.4043)	45
Charlie Gehringer	.404 (.4036)	46
Joe Cunningham	.404 (.4035)	47
Lu Blue	.402 (.4022)	48
Chipper Jones	.402 (.4017)	49
Joe Kelley	.402 (.4017)	50
Rickey Henderson	.401 (.4012)	51
Larry Walker	.400 (.4002)	52
Luke Appling	.399 (.3994)	53
Elmer Smith	.399 (.3988)	54
Tip O Neill	.399 (.3985)	55
Ross Youngs	.399 (.3985)	56
Joe DiMaggio	.398 (.3983)	57
Elmer Valo	.398 (.3983)	58
Gary Sheffield	.398 (.3981)	59
Ralph Kiner	.398 (.3980)	60
John Olerud	.398 (.3980)	61
Johnny Mize	.397 (.3971)	62

(cont.)

(cont.)

Roger Connor	.397 (.3970)	63
Earle Combs	.397 (.3969)	64
John Kruk	.397 (.3966)	65
Richie Ashburn	.396 (.3964)	66
Mike Hargrove	.396 (.3958)	67
Hack Wilson	.395 (.3951)	68
Earl Averill	.395 (.3947)	69
Cap Anson	.395 (.3945)	70
Johnny Pesky	.394 (.3943)	71
Mark McGwire	.394 (.3941)	72
Stan Hack	.394 (.3940)	73
Eddie Yost	.394 (.3940)	74
Frank Chance	.394 (.3937)	75
Ken Williams	.393 (.3933)	76
Wally Schang	.393 (.3931)	77
Rod Carew	.393 (.3930)	78
Mike Griffin	.393 (.3930)	79
Bob Johnson	.393 (.3928)	80
Bill Terry	.393 (.3927)	81
George Grantham	.392 (.3924)	82
Jack Fournier	.392 (.3921)	83
Joe Morgan	.392 (.3921)	84

Mike Tiernan	.392 (.3917)	85
Joe Sewell	.391 (.3909)	86
Honus Wagner	.391 (.3909)	87
Carlos Delgado	.390 (.3904)	88
Augie Galan	.390 (.3904)	89
Hughie Jennings	.390 (.3902)	90
Dave Magadan	.390 (.3902)	91
Harlond Clift	.390 (.3901)	92
Vladimir Guerrero	.390 (.3897)	93
Joe Cronin	.389 (.3895)	94
Buddy Myer	.389 (.3894)	95
Elmer Flick	.389 (.3890)	96
Frank Robinson	.389 (.3890)	97
Minnie Minoso	.389 (.3885)	98
Derek Jeter	.388 (.3884)	99
Dolph Camilli	.388 (.3883)	100

Base on Balls

All-Time Leaders
"Top 100"

NAME	BASE ON BALLS	RANK
Barry Bonds	2,426	1
Rickey Henderson	2,190	2
Babe Ruth	2,062	3
Ted Williams	2,021	4
Joe Morgan	1,865	5
Carl Yastrzemski	1,845	6
Mickey Mantle	1,733	7
Mel Ott	1,708	8
Eddie Yost	1,614	9
Darrell Evans	1,605	10
Stan Musial	1,599	11
Pete Rose	1,566	12
Harmon Killebrew	1,559	13
Frank Thomas	1,547	14
Lou Gehrig	1,508	15
Mike Schmidt	1,507	16
Eddie Collins	1,499	17
Willie Mays	1,464	18

Jimmie Foxx	1,452	19
Eddie Mathews	1,444	20
Frank Robinson	1,420	21
Wade Boggs	1,412	22
Hank Aaron	1,402	23
Jeff Bagwell	1,401	24
Dwight Evans	1,391	25
Tris Speaker	1,381	26
Reggie Jackson	1,375	27
Jim Thome	1,364	28
Rafael Palmeiro	1,353	29
Willie McCovey	1,345	30
Eddie Murray	1,333	31
Tim Raines	1,330	32
Tony Phillips	1,319	33
Mark McGwire	1,317	34
Fred McGriff	1,305	35
Luke Appling	1,302	36
Gary Sheffield	1,293	37
Edgar Martinez	1,283	38
Al Kaline	1,277	39
John Olerud	1,275	40

(cont.)

(cont.)

Ken Singleton	1,263	41
Jack Clark	1,262	42
Rusty Staub	1,255	43
Ty Cobb	1,249	44
Willie Randolph	1,243	45
Jimmy Wynn	1,224	46
Dave Winfield	1,216	47
Pee Wee Reese	1,210	48
Richie Ashburn	1,198	49
Brian Downing	1,197	50
Lou Whitaker	1,197	51
Chili Davis	1,194	52
Billy Hamilton	1,187	53
Charlie Gehringer	1,186	54
Donie Bush	1,158	55
Max Bishop	1,153	56
Toby Harrah	1,153	57
Craig Biggio	1,137	58
Harry Hooper	1,136	59
Jimmy Sheckard	1,135	60
Brett Butler	1,129	61
Cal Ripken, Jr.	1,129	62

Ron Santo	1,108	63
George Brett	1,096	64
Paul Molitor	1,094	65
Lu Blue	1,092	66
Stan Hack	1,092	67
Paul Waner	1,091	68
Jason Giambi	1,089	69
Graig Nettles	1,088	70
Bobby Grich	1,087	71
Ken Griffey, Jr.	1,077	72
Mark Grace	1,075	73
Bob Johnson	1,075	74
Robin Ventura	1,075	75
Ozzie Smith	1,072	76
Harlond Clift	1,070	77
Keith Hemandez	1,070	78
Chipper Jones	1,070	79
Bernie Williams	1,069	80
Bill Dahlen	1,064	81
Harold Baines	1,062	82
Joe Cronin	1,059	83
Luis Gonzalez	1,058	84

(cont.)

Manny Ramirez	1,054	85
Ron Fairly	1,052	86
Billy Williams	1,045	87
Norm Cash	1,043	88
Eddie Joost	1,043	89
Roy Thomas	1,042	90
Max Carey	1,040	91
Rogers Hornsby	1,038	92
Jim Gilliam	1,036	93
Roberto Alomar	1,032	94
Sal Bando	1,031	95
Jesse Burkett	1,029	96
Rod Carew	1,018	97
Enos Slaughter	1,018	98
Ron Cey	1,012	99
Ralph Kiner	1,011	100

BATTING GLOSSARY

BATTING AVGERAGE

A baseball player's batting average refers to the percentage of official at bats in which that player gets a base hit. A batting average of .300, for example, means that the player in question gets a base hit 30 percent of all the times he completes an official at bat.

Batting average is calculated by dividing the number of base hits a player has earned by his total number of at bats (H/AB) and rounding to three decimal places.

Also Known As: BA, average, avg.

ON-BASE PERCENTAGE

On-base percentage is a valuable statistic in determining a player's worth to his team. Put simply, OBP is the rate at which a given player gets on base during his at bats. In other words, OBP is the rate at which a player avoids making outs. Even if his batting average is low, he can still be a valuable hitter if his OBP is high.

To calculate OBP, add together a player's hits (H), walks (BB), and times hit by a pitch (HBP). Then divide that total by the sum of his at-bats (AB), BB, HBP, and sacrifice flies (SF). Then round to three decimal places.

Also Known As: OBP, OB%, on-base average

ON-BASE PLUS SLUGGING

On-base plus slugging (OPS) is a relatively new metric used to measure a player's ability both to get on base and hit for power, two of the most valuable assets to a team. Essentially, OPS is a combination of on-base percentage and slugging percentage.

To quickly calculate OPS, determine a player's OBP and SLG to three decimal places and then add the two numbers together. That will give you a very close approximation of OPS. To more accurately calculate OPS, use the following formula:

at bats (hits + walks + times hit by pitch) + total bases (at bats + sacrifice flies + walks + times hit by pitch) / at bats (at bats + sacrifice flies + walks + times hit by pitch)

SLUGGING PERCENTAGE

Slugging percentage is a valuable statistic in determining a player's ability to hit for power. Batting average measures what percentage of the time a batter gets a hit and on-base percentage measures a hitter's ability to avoid making outs, but slugging percentage takes into account how many bases the batter achieves with his hits.

To calculate SLG, add the total number of bases a batter's hits account for and divide by his total number of at bats and round to three decimal places. Here is a simple formula:

[(singles + (2 x doubles) + (3 x triples) + (4 x home runs)] / AB

Also Known As: SLG%, SL%, SLUG

Baseball Hitting Statistics

Year: Year in which the season occurred

Ag: Player age on July 1 of that year.

Tm: Team he played for

Lg: League he played in (AL- American League, NL- National League)

G: Games played

AB: At Bats

R: Runs Scored

H: Hits

2B: Doubles

3B: Triples

HR: Home Runs

RBI: Runs Batted In

BB: Base on Balls or Walks

SO: Strikeouts or K's

BA: Batting Average—H/AB

OBP: On-Base Percentage—H+BB+HBP / (AB+BB+SF+HBP) (SF and HBP are assumed zero if unavailable)

SLG: Slugging Percentage—TB/AB

TB: Total Bases—(singles + 2*2B + 3*3B + 4*HR)

SH: Sacrifice Hits or Bunts

SF: Sacrifice Flies

IBB: Intentional Base on Balls

HBP: Hit by Pitch

GDP or GIDP: Grounded into Double Plays

OPS: On-Base Percentage + Slugging Percentage

Miscellaneous Hitting Statistics

AB/HR: At Bats per Home Runs. A power ratio calculated by dividing the number of at bats by home runs hits.

AB/K: At Bats per Strikeouts. A success at the plate ratio calculated by dividing the number of at bats by strikeouts.

AB/RBI: At Bats per Runs Batted In. A scoring runs ratio that determines the number of runs batted in based on a players total at bats.

Basic Baseball Glossary

Balk: An illegal motion by the pitcher with one or more runners on base, entitling all runners to advance one base. A balk can be one of a number of movements related to the pitching motion but the intention is to catch the runners off balance.

Ball: A pitch that does not enter the strike zone and is not struck at by the batter.

Base: The four points of the baseball diamond (first through third bases and home plate) that must be touched by a runner in order to score a run.

Batter: The offensive player who is currently positioned in the batter's box.

Batter's Box: Either of the areas next to home plate where the batter stands during his time at bat.

Bunt: A legally batted ball, not swung at but intentionally met with the bat and tapped within the infield.

Catch: The act of a fielder in getting secure possession in his hand or glove of a ball in flight and firmly holding it.

Catcher: The defensive player whose position is directly behind home plate.

Defense: The team currently in the field.

Designated Hitter: A player who may be designated to bat instead of the pitcher.

Double: A play in which the batter makes it safely to second base without stopping.

Double Play: A defensive play in which two offensive players are put out as a result of one continuous action.

Fair Ball: A legally batted ball that settles on or over fair territory.

Fair Territory: The part of the playing field within and including the first base and third base lines, from home plate to the playing field fence and perpendicularly upward.

Fielder: One of the nine defensive players, including pitcher, catcher, first baseman, second baseman, third baseman, shortstop, left fielder, center fielder, and right fielder.

Fielder's Choice: The act of a fielder who handles a fair grounder and, instead of throwing to first base to put out the batter runner, throws to another base in an attempt to put out a preceding runner.

Fly Ball: A ball that goes high in the air when batted.

Force Play: A play in which a runner loses his right to occupy a base when the current batter becomes a runner.

Forfeited Game: A game declared ended by the umpire for violation of the rules, and awarded to the offended team.

Foul Ball: A batted ball that lands on foul territory between home plate and first base or third base, bounds past first or third base on or over third territory, first touches foul territory beyond first or third base, or touches a player, umpire, or any object not part of the playing field while over foul territory.

Foul Territory: That part of the playing field outside the first and third base lines extended to the outfield fence and perpendicularly upward.

Ground Ball: A batted ball which rolls along the ground.

Ground Rule Double: When a line drive bounces on the field and over the wall in fair territory the hit is scored as a ground rule double and the batter advances to second base.

Home Plate: The base over which an offensive player bats, and to which he must return after touching all three bases in order to score a run.

Home Run: A play in which the batter makes it safely around all bases and back to home plate without stopping.

Home Team: The team on whose field the game is played. If the game is played on neutral grounds, the home team shall be designated by mutual agreement.

Infield: The diamond-shaped portion of the playing field bordered by the four bases.

Infielder: A fielder who occupies a position in the infield.

Infield Fly: A fair fly ball that can be caught by an infielder with ordinary effort, which first and second, or first, second, and third bases are occupied before the second out. Infield Fly Rule: On the infield fly rule the umpire is to rule whether the ball could ordinarily have been handled by an infielder, not by some arbitrary limitation such as the grass, or the base lines. The umpire's judgment must govern, and the decision should be made immediately. When an infield fly rule is called, runners may advance at their own risk. If on an infield fly rule, the infielder intentionally drops a fair ball, the ball remains in play.

Inning: That portion of the game within which the teams alternate on offense and defense and in which there are three outs for each team. Each team's time at bat is a half-inning.

Line Drive: A ball that is batted directly to a fielder without touching the ground.

Out: A declaration by the umpire that a player who is trying for a base is not entitled to that base.

Outfield: The portion of the playing field that extends beyond the infield and is bordered by the first and third baselines.

Outfielder: A fielder who occupies a position in the outfield.

Pitch: The ball delivered by the pitcher to the batter.

Pitcher: The fielder designated to pitch the ball to the batter.

Quick Return Pitch: An illegal pitch, made with obvious intent to catch the batter off balance.

Run: The score made by an offensive player who has rounded the bases and returned to home plate.

Runner: An offensive player who is advancing toward, touching, or returning to any base.

Safe: A declaration by the umpire that a runner who is trying for a base has not been tagged or forced out, and is therefore entitled to that base.

Single: A play in which the batter safely makes it to first base.

Strike: A legal pitch when so called by the umpire, which:

1. Is struck at by the batter and missed;
2. Is not struck at, if the ball passes through the strike zone;
3. Is fouled by the batter when he has less than two strikes;
4. Is bunted foul;
5. Touches the batter as he strikes at it;
6. Touches the batter in flight in the strike zone; or
7. After being batted, travels directly from the bat to the catcher's hands and is legally caught by the catcher (foul tip).

Strike Zone: An area directly over home plate, from the bottom of the batter's kneecaps to the midpoint between the top of the batter's shoulders and the top of the batter's uniform pants.

Tag: The action of a fielder in touching a base with his body while holding the ball, or touching a runner with the ball, or with his hand or glove while holding the ball.

Throw: The act of propelling the ball toward a given objective, usually a teammate. A pitch is not a throw.

Top: The first half of an inning.

Triple: A play in which the batter makes it safely to third base without stopping.

Triple Play: A defensive play in which three offensive players are put out as a result of one action.

Umpire: The official who judges the legality of individual plays and who otherwise enforces the rules of the game.

MISCELLANEOUS BASEBALL HISTORY

1839 — Abner Doubleday is credited with inventing baseball in Cooperstown, New York.

1846 — The first official game of baseball is played between the Knickerbockers and a group of cricket players.

1867 — Candy Cummings throws the first curveball in baseball.

1876 — The National League is established, with William Hulbert as president.

1900 — The American League is created.

1903 — The Boston Pilgrims and the Pittsburgh Pirates play the first World Series.

1912 — Fenway Park opens.

1919 — In the most famous scandal in baseball history, eight players from the Chicago White Sox are accused of throwing the World Series against the Cincinnati Reds.

1920 — Babe Ruth is sold to the New York Yankees.

1925 — Lou Gehrig replaces Wally Pipp in the Yankee lineup.

1927 — The 1927 Yankees are considered one of the greatest baseball teams of all time.

1932 — Babe Ruth hits his legendary "called shot" home run against Charlie Root and the Chicago Cubs.

— Lou Gehrig hits four home runs in one game.

1933 — Major League Baseball's first All-Star game is played.

1941 — Joe DiMaggio hits safely in 56 consecutive games.
— Ted Williams hits .406 for the season.

1945 — Jackie Robinson makes his Major League debut.

1951 — Bobby Thomson hits his pennant-winning home run against the Dodgers.

1961 — Roger Maris breaks Babe Ruth's home run record.

1973 — George Steinbrenner buys the New York Yankees.
— The designated hitter rule is established in the American League.

1974 — Hank Aaron breaks Babe Ruth's career home run record.

1985 — Pete Rose breaks Ty Cobb's all-time hit record.

1988 — Kirk Gibson hits a pinch-hit game-winning home run in the World Series.

1995 — Cal Ripken Jr. breaks Lou Gehrig's streak with his 2,131st consecutive game.

NAME INDEX

Dear Fellow Hitmen,

I am very excited to share with you all the hitting experience gathered during my baseball career, initially as a MLB Player and now as a coach. My coaching career really started with my sons and their friends in youth baseball and now extends to Major League players. My dream is to enable each and every ballplayer to develop proper batting techniques which will have them hitting at the highest level consistent with their ability. Hitting is my passion and I created this book to capture, the step-by-step hitting mechanics I've learned over the years. Additionally, I've gone one step further and created a batting technology especially designed to transfer the strength generated by your whole body into maximized bat head velocity through the strike zone. For the past decade, I have been perfecting what I call V-Grip™ technology for the handle of the bat. Without the proper grip, high-quality, scientifically engineered bats alone do little to enhance swing performance – your bat head will lag through the hitting zone losing speed, power and control thereby reducing your ability to consistently hit a strike-zone ball. The patented V-Grip™ allows you to immediately maximize the power of your swing by placing the bat – first time and every time – in the proper hitting position during your swing.

Knocking Knuckle Alignment   Away from Palm into Fingertips

ADULT BASEBALL
Aluminum

Wood

Maple

Ash

Hickory

SENIOR LEAGUE BASEBALL
Aluminum

TRAIN & GAME™ PACKAGE
Wood/Aluminum

The company I created, Mattingly Baseball, brings you the world's first bat that actually improves hitting technique. A Mattingly V-Grip™ bat provides proven performance which helps a hitter deliver the bat's sweet spot to the ball over and over again. Only the V-Grip™ is specifically designed to keep the knocker knuckles aligned and shift the bat away from the palm and into the fingers – correctly "power-loading" your energy, allowing your grip to be in

YOUTH BASEBALL
Aluminum

TEE BALL
Aluminum

SLOW-PITCH SOFTBALL
Aluminum

Wood

Maple

Ash

Hickory

Poplar

FAST-PITCH SOFTBALL
Aluminum

perfect alignment every time for perfect follow-through. The V-Grip™ bat has a stiff tapered handle which transfers more energy than other manufacturers' flexible "whip" handle to promote power at the point of impact. I have created an entire line of league certified wood and aluminum V-Grip™ bats from Tee Ball to Youth to Adult Fast-Pitch, Slow-Pitch, and even Softball that I would like to share with you.

Batting Gloves

Caps

Apparel

Bat Bags

As we move forward, we at Mattingly Baseball are committed to becoming the leaders of innovation in baseball and softball equipment. We have begun a line of batting gloves and bat bags to complement the V-Grip™ bats. We intend to tap into the latent innovation that exists in the baseball and softball world and deliver additional products to the market which will demonstrably improve the skills of today's players.

Here's to becoming the best player you can be!

Don Mattingly

Don Mattingly

For More Product Information or to Order visit:
www.MattinglyBaseball.com